"What makes a good parent? In a maste
their immense clinical experience to prov
for parents attempting to do what is best
volume to apply well-established principl
parents to overcome the emotional obstacl
book not only for parents but for all mental health professionals."

> —Aaron T. Beck, M.D., University Professor of Psychiatry,
> University of Pennsylvania School of Medicine

"In a boldly innovative approach, Drs. Elliott and Smith have written a book that is sure to become a classic parenting resource. In it they teach parents how to change the way they think so they can rise to every challenge in their children's development. Through a series of very engaging and realistic stories, the authors usher readers through the process of identifying their core beliefs, understanding their impact on parenting style, and building the skills that help them reach their goals. And all of this is accomplished by building on parents' skills rather than shaming them for their weaknesses."

> —Richard B. Stuart, D.S.W., Clinical Psychologist, Former
> President, Association for the Advancement of Behavior
> Therapy

"Drs. Elliot and Smith have written a unique book for parents who are frustrated by their own parenting behavior. While many parenting books focus on the behavioral techniques that parents can use to change their children's behavior, this book concentrates on the cognitive strategies that parents will find invaluable in helping them understand their actions. All too often, parents know what is the right thing to do, but don't do it at the time of a parenting opportunity. This book clearly describes the many cognitive "schemas" that often interfere with effective parenting, and provides multiple informative case illustrations of schemas in everyday parenting experiences. This highly readable book will be useful for all parents who find that in spite of knowing what to do, they time after time fail to achieve their vision of effective parenting."

> —Dr. James W. Varni is Professor of Psychiatry at the University
> of California, San Diego, School of Medicine and author of
> *Time-Out for Toddlers*

"Although there are indeed a large number of self-help books on the market today for troubled parents, I was deeply impressed with *Why Can't I Be the Parent I Want to Be?* It is one of the few—perhaps the only—that addresses a fundamental and critical issue in parenting, specifically, that many well-intended and loving parents know good parenting practice, but cannot implement or put into practice such skills because of their own emotional barriers. From this perspective, *Why Can't I Be the Parent I Want to Be?* offers an opportunity for parents to reach beyond technique-oriented parenting. The use of rich examples brings the book alive as the reader is invited along on each family's journey of self-discovery. The stories allow for an elegant, yet clear means of understanding the model and concepts. In summary, I think this book is a wonderful addition to the parenting literature."

—Larry L. Mullins, Ph.D., Associate Professor of Psychology, Oklahoma State University

"*Why Can't I Be the Parent I Want to Be?* sensitively portrays the plight of so many parents who truly want to be more effective parents, but somehow can't break free of old patterns of discipline and communication with their children. While there are many self-help books on the market that do an excellent job of explaining effective discipline techniques, this is the only book I know of that focuses on the more subtle processes that get in the way of implementing good discipline methods. By demonstrating how schemas can distort parents' perceptions and result in automatic and less than ideal reactions to children's behavior, the authors help parents better understand and accept why they may have had so much trouble altering their parenting practices in the past. Even more importantly, however, the authors provide detailed recommendations and practical exercises to help parents change schemas and implement more effective parenting strategies."

—Lyndha Dahlquist, Ph.D., Associate Professor, University of Maryland, Baltimore County

"Drs. Elliott and Smith explain how parenting patterns can unwittingly trap you or free you to be the parent you want to be. The book presents entertaining and educational portraits of real parents and kids struggling with real problems. The authors offer realistic suggestions to put an end to unintentional but destructive parent-child interactions."

—Maureen Kirby Lassen, Ph.D., Faculty, The Fielding Institute, co-author of *Why Can't I Get What I Want?* and author of *Why are We Still Fighting?*

"Parenting is a tough job. Understanding how to parent is even tougher. Young people in correction facilities represent the worst outcome of parenting gone astray. This book, through the use of new psychological findings provides profound insights into how parents' emotions and behaviors impact their relationship with their children. Examine it. Review it. Relish every word. You will be surprised by how you can change your parenting in a way that will produce positive and meaningful relationships with your children."

—Eduardo B. Soto, Principle, Albuquerque Public Schools, Juvenile Detention Center

Why Can't I Be the Parent I Want to Be?

END OLD PATTERNS AND ENJOY YOUR CHILDREN

Charles H. Elliott, Ph.D.
Laura L. Smith, Ph.D.

Foreword by John Rosemond

New Harbinger Publications, Inc.

Distributed in the U.S.A. by Publishers Group West; in Canada by Raincoast Books; in Great Britain by Airlift Book Company, Ltd.; in South Africa by Real Books, Ltd.; in Australia by Boobook; and in New Zealand by Tandem Press.

Copyright © 1999 by Charles H. Elliott, Ph.D., and Laura L. Smith, Ph.D.
New Harbinger Publications, Inc.
5674 Shattuck Avenue
Oakland, CA 94609

Cover design by Blue Design
Author photo by Karen Villanueva Photography © 1999-2000
Edited by Angela Watrous
Text design by Tracy Marie Powell

Library of Congress Catalog Card Number: 99-74373
ISBN 1-57224-171-3 Paperback

All Rights Reserved

Printed in the United States of America.

New Harbinger Publications' Website address: www.newharbinger.com

01   00   99

10   9   8   7   6   5   4   3   2   1

First printing

ACKNOWLEDGMENTS

This book represents a marriage of the fields of education and psychology. We appreciate all of those who contributed to our professional training and development, including the faculties at the University of Kansas, Wayne State University, the University of New Mexico, and the Fielding Institute.

We are especially grateful to our editor, Angela Watrous, for her careful, thoughtful work and an eye for detail we could never hope to match. In addition, we owe gratitude to our friends, colleagues, and families who supported our efforts in many ways. They read various drafts of our work, encouraged us, and forgave us for our neglect. And finally, we thank Trevor for his tolerance of the evenings we spent in front of the computer.

We dedicate this book to our families, old and new—especially to our children and our parents, who provided us with challenges, practice, pain, and joy. We also dedicate this book to love, and to the dream we share.

Contents

FOREWORD

"Why Can't I Be the Parent I Want to Be?" will surprise and delight you. The authors teach the old-fashioned way—with stories. You'll follow three families through their efforts to become better parents. The families' stories poignantly illustrate the authors' ideas in dramatic scenes. As you read about these families, you may laugh or you may cry. You will be touched. The authors, Charles Elliott and Laura Smith, have written a wonderful self-help book. Quite unique in that it entertains as well as it teaches.

Who should read this book? Perhaps you are a parent who has attended one of my workshops, followed my columns, or read some of my books. You are one of those who listens to or reads my ideas while nodding your head in enthusiastic agreement. You return home to those kids with the great intention of changing the way you parent. But something stops you. You find yourself returning to old habits: not setting limits, caving in to tantrums, or expecting too little from your kids. If so, this book is for you.

This book is also for you if you believe in common-sense parenting. Readers familiar with my work know that I believe parenting is a matter of common sense. Yet, many parents find it impossible to do what is right for their children. Permissive parents create spoiled children, children who lack responsibility and ambition, who are self-centered and lack character. I have blamed the psychobabble of permissive professionals for fostering the spoiling of our children. But that's only part of the problem.

"Why Can't I Be the Parent I Want to Be?" explains why parents fail to implement common-sense notions of parenting. As the authors note, the parent in your heart knows how to parent. All too often, parents fail to do what they know is right. Why? Emotional obstacles caused by entrenched beliefs prevent parents form following through on their good intentions. The authors call these beliefs schemas, a slight indulgence in psycho-babble. They can be forgiven for a few departures from my approach because the book is written with a clarity and creative flare not usually found in self-help books.

—John Rosemond
Psychologist

Chapter 1

THE PARENTING PUZZLE

The Obstacle to Good Parenting

Why Parents Need More Than Advice

You already know *how* to parent. Most parents understand the essentials of good parenting. The parent existing in your heart knows kids thrive on love and affection, appropriate praise, reasonable limits, protection from harm when needed, and expectations for good behavior. And you know they don't need icy coldness, spoiling, derisive criticism, intense pressure, and so on.

Yet, parents usually *think* they need more advice on *how* to parent. It's a real puzzle because most parents actually know *exactly* what to do, they just can't get themselves to do it. We call this phenomenon the Parenting Puzzle—knowing what you should do, but finding yourself unable to do it. It explains why parents ask, "Why can't I be the parent I want to be?"

The Parenting Puzzle is at work whenever you do any of the following:

- give in to your kids' whining
- lose your temper
- overprotect your kids
- criticize your kids too much
- make excuses for your kids
- set excessive standards for your kids
- rarely have fun with your kids

Perhaps you see yourself as having difficulty with one or more of these issues from time to time. If so, you're ahead of the game because some parents with these habits don't even recognize that there is a problem. Changing your parenting style includes learning to recognize problems. But it also involves changing the obstacles and emotions that lie behind them.

For several decades, cognitive-behavioral therapy has provided powerful tools for overcoming emotional obstacles. Through strategies based on the latest cognitive-behavioral therapy principles, we'll teach you to identify the internal forces that control your parenting. Then, whenever you find yourself stuck, you will know why you are stuck and what to do about it. And you'll learn how to use the Middle Way of Parenting for calming chaos when it arises. But, this is not another book on *how to parent*. Dozens of books stand ready to give you more "how-to" advice than this one will. The Parenting Puzzle is that parents often know exactly how they should parent but nevertheless end up unable to be the parent they want to be. This book will help you find the parent that already exists in your heart.

We think you'll find this book enjoyable. We're presenting most of our material within the context of stories. Stories have been used since ancient times to teach, and they make learning fun. We will follow three families through their quest for change. You probably won't find yourself identically portrayed by one of our characters, but you will likely relate to their hopes, fears, dreams, vulnerabilities, and humanness. And you'll learn from their struggles as they grapple with adversity, unexpected events, frustration, hope, and change.

Schemas: The Key to the Parenting Puzzle

Children constantly try to make sense of themselves and their world. Information bombards them nonstop. As infants they see light, darkness, faces, colors; they hear music, voices, barking, cars, and noise; they smell milk, mother, powder; they touch blankets, bath water, stuffed animals, and people; they are wrapped in blankets, rocked, or left alone. At first it's all chaos. But even within the first few hours of life, the newborn learns to recognize a human face as more than blobs of dark and light. In a matter of days, infants recognize and respond with pleasure to their mothers' faces.

This miraculous process of organizing and creating meaning out of the world involves what psychologists call forming schemas. Schemas categorize and organize information. They provide a shortcut to recognition and understanding. Can you imagine if every time you saw a pair of eyes, a nose, and a mouth, you had to ask yourself, "Hmm, what has two eyes, a nose, and a mouth? Oh, I guess it's a face!" The human brain, like a computer, can instantaneously process information through the formation of schemas.

Schemas classify a wide range of information into categories. People form schemas about the sequence of events which allow them to carry out complex routines without thinking much about it. For example, you have probably driven home from work without paying attention to how you're getting there. Most likely, you followed the traffic laws, navigated a series of turns and maneuvers, and made it home safely. By contrast, when you first started driving, you had no schema to guide you. A new driver must think about every action, from turning the wheel to stepping on the brake. After hundreds of repetitions, driving becomes automatic. In a sense, you have formed a "driving" schema.

Schemas also help people create meaning about who they are. Such information doesn't just come from textbooks and teachers. It comes from a smile or a pat on the back when you have done well, cruel teasing on the playground, or an older sibling's scorn. Society and the people around you provide millions of pieces of data from which you form the schemas you have about yourself.

Such schemas are a set of beliefs and feelings about yourself and your relationship to other people. They govern how you feel about who you are and about the people around you. And they influence almost everything you do, think, or feel.

People form schemas during childhood as a way to make sense out of their world. Schemas are normal and natural reactions to events. However, once formed, it can be difficult not to hold on to them when your world has changed. In other words, a schema may be adaptive when it's created, but when it continues into adulthood, it can cause big problems if it no longer fits. It behooves parents to understand this powerful force over their lives.

This force can dramatically affect your parenting. Schemas answer the Parenting Puzzle by explaining why parents struggle to be the parent they want to be. Earlier we gave you an example of a "driving" schema. You saw how such a schema makes driving virtually automatic. Schemas related to parenting can also make your parenting run on a thoughtless, autopilot mode. Below, we've listed the most common schemas that affect parenting. You'll learn more about them in chapters to come.

- Anxious-Attachment schema: I greatly fear losing others.
- Blameworthy schema: Guilt is my middle name.
- Naive schema: I think everything always works out.

- Other-Centered schema: Others' needs take center stage while my own needs are neglected.
- Pefectionistic schema: Everything and everyone has to be perfect.
- No Play schema: I don't believe in fun and relaxation.
- Excessive-Control schema: I discipline to excess.
- Avoidant-Attachment schema: I avoid intimacy and closeness.
- Blameless schema: It's never my fault and my children can do no wrong.
- Distrust schema: The world is out to get me or my children.
- Self-Centered schema: I focus on my own needs and neglect those of others.
- Unambitious schema: I could care less about achievement.
- All Play schema: I put play and recreation above all else.
- No Control schema: I can't set limits.

Later in this chapter we'll discuss how schemas are formed in more detail. But first, let's meet two of the families we'll be following throughout the book. Later we'll explain how their schemas are getting in the way of their parenting.

Kenneth, Sally, Lindsey, and Nick

Six o'clock. Boiling water spills and hisses over the sides of the full pot of pasta. Kenneth sighs loudly as annoyance floods over him. "Damn it, your mother is still not home. We might as well eat." For Kenneth, life has not been the same since his wife, Sally, took a new job. He feels it hardly pays her enough to justify the inconvenience it causes him. He can't believe she expects him to take over dinner and the kids every time she's late.

Ten-year-old Nick, sprawled on the floor in front of the blaring TV, looks up from his homework. "Hold on, Dad. I just have two more problems to finish."

Kenneth, fed up, grabs the hot handles of the pot and splashes pasta into the colander. "Dinner is ready now! You should have started your homework earlier. How can you possibly concentrate with that stupid boob tube blasting? And where's your sister?"

"She's where she always is—on the phone."

"For God's sake, get your sister and come to the table *now*," he shouts.

"Really, Dad. Chill out." Thirteen-year-old Lindsey strolls in, rolling her eyes at her brother, cordless phone still attached to her ear.

"Don't you talk to me that way, young lady. I don't know where you got that smart mouth, but I won't stand for it. Just close it and get to the table. This family will eat together when I say so."

Lindsey flips her blond ponytail. "Oh boy, I can hardly wait. Come on, Nick, let's have some quality family time."

"Lindsey, if you spent half as much time on your homework as you do on the phone or talking back to me, maybe you'd get decent grades like your brother." Kenneth turns as his wife walks in.

"I don't care what you think—you make me sick," Lindsey says, stung by her father's comments.

Sally's smile collapses as she walks into another family squabble. "Lindsey, I've told you not to talk to your father like that."

Kenneth snaps at his wife, "You don't need to rescue me. I can handle these kids." The family sits down to a silent dinner.

As he looks around at his unhappy family, Kenneth feels confused. Sally rarely gets into fights with the kids. He knows something is wrong. Why doesn't Lindsey listen to him without all that sarcasm? He'd really like to be close to his kids. He's beginning to realize his temper and tough style don't seem to work in this family. He'd like to change but can't seem to pull it off. Even when he knows what to say, the words refuse to come out. Why can't he be the parent that he wants to be?

Has this ever happened to you? Have you known what you *should* do in parenting your child, yet been unable to do it, ending up sounding like your own mother or father? Or maybe you don't act at all like your own parents, but still can't break out of your bad parenting habits. You want to do something better, but nothing you try seems to work over time. Do you find yourself spewing out hateful words and immediately feeling remorse? Or do you valiantly struggle to set limits and boundaries with your kids, and ultimately cave in? Do you overindulge your kids sometimes and overreact at other times? Who seems to be in charge of your emotions—you or your kid? If you aren't happy with your answers to these questions, you're not alone. Let's look at Jennifer's situation another example of a parent who can't seem to be the parent she wants to be.

Jennifer and Jerod

Jennifer Dearborn sits nervously in children's court, straightening her skirt, and practicing the deep breathing her counselor taught her. It doesn't help this time. She attempts to catch the eye of her son's attorney, but he's preoccupied with another boy's case. To pass the time, Jennifer focuses her attention on the drama of the other case.

The attorney looks bored; it's his tenth hearing of the day. He's heard these sad sagas too many times. The judge questions the boy, who mumbles some words about how he'll change. The boy's mother speaks rapidly, making promises, while her son stands sullenly at her side. "Your Honor, I will make sure my son gets to school everyday. I will keep him away from that bad group of kids he's been hanging around with. He won't be using any more drugs and I won't let him out of my sight."

Jennifer remembers her first appearance in children's court—still hopeful and making the same promises to the judge. She'd been so sure the threat of jail time posed by the judge would scare her son, Jerod, into cleaning up his act. With Jerod now facing a second stint in the detention center, the illusion of his being "scared straight" has faded. She wonders, "What went wrong? I've tried so hard to be a good parent—different from my own parents, who never had time for me and worked constantly. It seemed like they didn't have time to love me, but I adore Jerod and he knows it. I worked extra hours to buy him whatever he wanted. I cooked him good meals. I cleaned his room. And when things started to go bad, we both went to counseling. I've tried to be a good parent. Why do I have a bad kid?" Jennifer glances at her watch thinking of how she'll lose another half day's pay for the second time this month.

The side door opens and a new group of children shuffle in, accompanied by an armed guard. The sight of her son in shackles still stuns Jennifer. A few of the kids look on the verge of tears. Others exude toughness and nonchalance. Jerod smiles confidently when he sees his mom. After all, he's only here for a minor probation violation. He ditched school, smoked a little pot, and later failed the random urine test required by his probation officer. Everyone knows the jails and detention centers are filled beyond capacity with kids who have far more serious offenses than his.

The bailiff calls Jerod's name. Jennifer quickly walks up to stand next to her son. Again, he smiles. She can't bring herself to return his smile and looks at the floor to keep from crying. She focuses so hard on maintaining control that she barely hears the voices of the attorney and the probation officer as they discuss her son's future.

"Mrs. Dearborn do you agree to these terms?" the judge inquires.

Jennifer shudders. "I'm sorry, Your Honor, what did you say those terms were?"

The judge leans forward, surprised at her inattentiveness. His voice rises sternly. "Mrs. Dearborn, I am releasing your son to your custody. I expect you to get him to his probation officer weekly. He will have random drug checks and attend the court's drug treatment program for six months."

"No," Jennifer's voice quivers. The courtroom stills. Probation officers and attorneys look up from their papers. Spectators momentarily forget their own concerns.

The judge scrutinizes Jennifer. "What did you say?"

"No," she repeats.

Jerod's confident demeanor suddenly cracks. "Mom? Mom, what are you saying? Mom, I love you."

"I will not get him to his probation officer weekly or to his random drug tests or to the court drug treatment program. I will not and cannot take custody of my son. He's all yours." Jennifer turns from the judge, striding out of the courtroom with tears streaming down her face.

Jennifer isn't a bad parent. She loves her son. She tried to do everything right for Jerod. She sacrificed an active social life and hundreds of dollars on therapy. When the counselor suggested new things to try, she listened eagerly. And then for some inexplicable reason, she found herself unable to implement the ideas. She had such a hard time setting the limits the counselor advised. Jennifer had always struggled to say no to Jerod, even when he was little. She knew what to do, she just couldn't do it. Why can't she be the parent she wants to be?

How Schemas Are Formed

Let's go back to Jennifer's childhood to illustrate how schemas develop. Keep in mind the vignette below represents a fraction of the experiences that actually went into creating Jennifer's schemas.

Ten-year-old Jennifer straightened her skirt nervously as she sat in the train station, even though this was her second trip to Camp Longlake. That year she was to attend the entire six-week session. She fought back tears.

"Quit fidgeting, Jennifer. Don't be such a baby. You're impossible sometimes. Camp is a great experience for a child. You should appreciate what we're doing for you. And you won't have to put up with your parents for most of the summer." Jennifer's mom looked at her watch, anxious to get on with her day unencumbered by her daughter.

"If you let me stay home, I promise I won't get in your way. You wouldn't even have to take care of me. I could just stay at home for the summer." She paused. Her mother's silence answered her request. "Mom? Why didn't Daddy come to the station to say good-bye?"

"Don't whine like that. You know how busy he is. Your father has important business. He can't be bothered with silly good-byes."

Jennifer's parents were always busy with their own lives. They constantly left her with baby-sitters or shipped her off to camp. Having a child seemed like an imposition dictated by societal expectations. Her parents' lack of connection and disinterest led Jennifer to feel anxious, abandoned, lonely, and unloved. She searched for signs that they might really love her but rarely found them. Thus, Jennifer formed a schema about herself we call Anxious-Attachment. People with an Anxious-Attachment schema typically believe that the important people in their lives either leave or become emotionally unavailable to them. Therefore, they work desperately to cling or hold on to relationships. Their intensity often overwhelms those close to them. Paradoxically, this anxious style can be perceived as smothering to the recipient, who ultimately rebels by ending or limiting the relationship. Sadly, like many of those with the Anxious-Attachment schema, Jennifer found that those closest to her eventually pulled away.

Jennifer has many other schemas about herself and her world. Despite her parents' self-centeredness, she tried hard to win their approval and attention. She fervently looked for ways to please them. She excelled in school, obeyed all their rules, and kept her room meticulously clean. She fashioned elaborate cards for them on holidays and birthdays, hoping for some response. Usually her parents received the cards with a casual glance and a perfunctory word of thanks. A couple of times they forgot her birthday, but she never complained. Jennifer came to believe that other people's needs were more important than her own.

This belief reflects another schema she acquired during childhood—Other-Centered. An Other-Centered schema entails the belief that other people's needs take center stage. One's own needs take a backseat. At the extreme, people with an Other-Centered schema rarely express their own wants or desires for fear of offending others. Much of their emotional lives focus on taking care of other people.

Jennifer's reaction to her parents' behavior was a common one. However, we also want you to know that sometimes people develop quite different schemas from similar experiences. We'll explain how that works in a later chapter.

Kenneth, the tyrannical father of Lindsey and Nick, also developed a variety of schemas during childhood. His father was a sales representative who felt deep inadequacies about himself. His modest income frustrated him profoundly. And he took his negative self-image out on his family.

Sitting in the duck blind with his father and older brother, nine-year-old Kenneth shivered from both fear and cold. He clung to his steaming cup of hot chocolate, but it did nothing to warm his hands or calm his concerns. Sunlight was barely creeping over the horizon. The sound of quacking ducks flying in from the north broke the silence.

"For once in your life hold the shotgun to your shoulder and at least point it toward the ducks, Kenneth," his father quietly growled. He put the duck call to his lips and made sounds that didn't particularly sound like ducks to Kenneth, though it seemed to work. The ducks descended toward the lake's unbroken surface. "Now."

In one smooth motion, Kenneth's father and brother stood, raised their guns to their shoulders, aimed, and fired. Two ducks dropped from the sky. Kenneth clumsily hauled the shotgun loosely to his shoulder. The kickback of the gun caused the barrel to jerk upward and the shot headed only remotely in the direction of the ducks. Kenneth stumbled backward and felt pain not only from the force of the gun on his shoulder, but from the humiliation of yet another miserable failure. Taking a moment from congratulating Kenneth's brother, their father turned. "Kenneth, how do you ever expect to be a hunter? Toughen up, kid. Your brother could shoot by the time he was seven. I'm not going to take you hunting anymore unless you at least try to shoot a gun the right way."

Kenneth fought back tears, knowing that if he cried, both his Dad and brother would tease him unmercifully. "Damn dog," he said. "He's what made me screw up." Kenneth kicked angrily at the dirt in front of the dog. Startled, the dog bolted.

Strife and conflict had always riddled Kenneth's family. His father was the unquestioned boss, and no one dared object. Even his favored older brother sometimes ended up on the receiving end of one of his father's tirades. Kenneth only got approval from his father when he won at something, whether it was a game of softball or a neighborhood fight.

Kenneth developed a particularly strong Excessive-Control schema in reaction to his father's abuse. An Excessive-Control schema compels a person to dominate others. Often it helps hide a sense of inadequacy. When not in charge, Kenneth feels unsafe and vulnerable. You've certainly met people like this. They are bossy, arrogant, always know what's right, and disregard other people's feelings, sometimes to the point of abuse. Kenneth's schema was born from his father's unrealistic expectations and mean-spirited behavior toward him. It was the only response young Kenneth knew how to make. However, as we shall see, Kenneth continues to carry this schema into adulthood. In childhood, Kenneth's schema helped him survive in his environment. As an adult, the schema no longer works and even Kenneth is beginning to sense the trouble it causes.

Kenneth's schemas developed automatically. Your schemas also developed automatically. Again, they simply reflect the brain's attempt to organize and make sense out of the world and yourself. For example, if your parents frequently criticized you as a child, you likely developed a schema such as Blameworthy. Why? As a child, you reasonably learned to expect to be blamed for most everything you did. As a child, you concluded you were at fault. After all, your parents gave you that message. Now, as an adult, you may feel you're to blame for things that aren't really your fault, such as when your kids bring home bad grades. Guilt stalks you like a bounty hunter in search of an escaped convict. You probably question your own parenting whenever your child errs, even if you had nothing to do with it.

If you were raised in a home by parents who worked constantly and disapproved of frivolity and fun, you could easily develop a No Play schema. That schema could drive you relentlessly, never allowing you to indulge in recreation and relaxation. You too might come to value work above all else. You don't have a choice about developing schemas. You must attempt to make sense out of your world. Having problematic schemas doesn't make you crazy or weird, they simply mean you learned to cope with your childhood experiences.

When you learn more about how schemas work, they become more understandable. Schemas perform like computer software. The same input into two different types of programs will result in completely different output. Pressing the "enter" key in one software program will cause a paragraph to shift, whereas in another it could put you into a new document. Data is interpreted quite differently by different software. So it is with schemas. Each schema works like a program with its own rules for interpreting and reacting to information.

With what little you know about Kenneth's and Jennifer's schemas, how would they react if someone criticized them? Most likely, Kenneth would see the criticism as unjustified and respond with anger and attack, while Jennifer would see herself as at fault and cave in. Same input, completely different interpretations. That's what schemas do.

If each person just had one schema, we could predict with great accuracy how people would respond to almost everything. We would just determine that particular schema and then we'd know. But it's a little more complicated because everyone has more than one schema. Let's look at another one of Jennifer's schemas in the stages of its early development.

As the handsome caterer in black and white passed around appetizers, nine-year-old Jennifer's mother surveyed the party. She was pleased that the city councilman and his wife were in animated conversation with her husband. The expensive floral decorations perfectly complemented the lavish furnishings of the house. She whispered to the caterer that it was time to summon Jennifer.

Jennifer's baby-sitter brushed her long brown hair. "Don't worry, honey, you look beautiful. You'll do just fine. Just relax and play like you did for me. No one out there can play the piano like you can."

"I'm so scared. Mommy gets really mad when I mess up. You remember the last party when I started to play and I froze up, don't you? Mommy wouldn't talk to me for a week. And you know Daddy. He hardly talks to me anyway. I'm so scared, I just really want to do good."

"It's time, Jennifer," the caterer called from the hallway.

The baby-sitter gave her a quick hug. "Go on now, you'll do great."

Jennifer sat down at the baby grand. Her mother smiled nervously as her father turned away to resume his conversation with the councilman.

Because her parents doled out approval so sparingly, Jennifer came to believe she had to be perfect in order to please them. Jennifer acquired the Perfectionist schema. Even her best performances fell short in her own eyes. Jennifer's parents were so preoccupied with themselves that they actually cared only that Jennifer didn't embarrass them. But Jennifer thought if she could just do well enough, some crumbs of approval might come her way. So Jennifer excelled in school. She developed into a talented pianist and she obsessed over her clothes and appearance. When she graduated from college summa cum laude, she only applied for positions well beneath her talents. She lacked the confidence to go after better jobs. She gave up the piano during high school because the pressure of performing tormented her to the breaking point. Even though she was intelligent and attractive, she pursued men beset with a host of problems. She never felt good enough for anyone else. Jennifer's schemas clouded her vision like a comfortable pair of glasses in need of a new prescription.

In fact, one of the best ways to think about schemas is to imagine them as a set of lenses through which you view the world and yourself. Sometimes the lens is clear, and other times it is rose colored, gray, cracked, or badly distorted. At times your glasses allow you to see better, while other times they blur your vision. Jennifer remains unaware that she looks at the world through these lenses, so they control her life outside of awareness. She believes, like most people, that the way she sees herself and the world is the only possible view.

Let's take a look at another one of Kenneth's schemas and how it developed. We will present you with a typical scene from Kenneth's childhood. Over the course of many such scenes, his schema developed.

The boys tumbled out of bed, laughed, and ran downstairs to open their presents on Christmas morning.

"Slow down. Stop running. What do you think this is, a playground? I don't want to spend Christmas in some emergency room because you kids fall down the stairs running around like maniacs," Kenneth's father bellowed.

The laughter died as Kenneth and his brother reached the bottom of the stairs. "Can we open our presents now, Dad?" Kenneth pleaded.

Kenneth had already spied the large package under the tree. He was sure that it contained the often asked for and promised train set.

"Everyone sit down. We are going to do this in an orderly fashion. I will pass out the presents one at a time. And don't be tearing the wrapping off. We can use it again next year," Kenneth's father barked while pulling his plaid robe across his bulging midsection. Stifling their excitement, the boys sat at attention on the couch. The first present was passed to Kenneth's brother. He got a new Remington twelve-gauge shotgun. "Thanks,

Dad, thanks. This is what I really wanted. Now I'll be able to shoot at least half as good you can."

Kenneth's father patted his favored son on the back. "You shoot pretty great right now. Let's plan a trip together the first weekend of hunting season, son."

He handed a small package to Kenneth, who hid his disappointment. But his hopes for the train set suddenly rose as he carefully peeled the wrapping away. It was a book all about the history of trains. "Thanks, Dad. I wonder what else I'll get?"

His dad continued passing out presents one at a time to the family. The large present remained alone, unopened under the tree.

"This is a special present for you, Kenneth. It's something I think the whole family can enjoy. I want you to know it cost a lot more money than I can really afford. I know you're not much of a sportsman, I guess you're just too clumsy for guns."

Kenneth squirmed with eager anticipation, oblivious to the cutting remark. He knew the train set awaited inside the wrapping.

"Now Kenneth, I told you not to rip the paper. Slow down. You could knock over the tree if you keep that up."

Kenneth's face fell as he choked back tears, "It's an encyclopedia set. Thanks, Dad."

Many such events led Kenneth to develop a Distrust schema. Among other things, Kenneth's dad and brother had often played cruel tricks on him for their own amusement. People who have this schema believe that things rarely work out the way they want or the way they should. Life is seen as fraught with disappointments. Most people are not to be trusted. One has to vigilantly survey the world for possible dangers.

So, what does all of this have to do with parenting? We believe parents can't stop making the same old mistakes until they become aware of the forces causing them in the first place. Schemas represent the key to understanding why you parent like you do.

Schema Lenses

People look at the world through their schemas, their "lenses," and they see only what their lenses allow them to see. Information can come through relatively intact, distorted, or completely filtered out just like sunglasses filter out UV rays. Now let's look at how these lenses work and how they relate to parenting.

Kenneth and Jennifer are parents who have trouble with their kids. Their schemas act as lenses through which they see their children. When seen through these lenses, their reactions become understandable. Not necessarily correct, but certainly understandable.

Kenneth believes he should dominate others, he needs to be in charge. Otherwise, he feels uncomfortable and vulnerable. People with this Excessive-Control schema almost always believe they're right in any situation. Jennifer's Other-Centered schema is that other people's needs always come first.

Read table 1.1, noticing how the different lenses cause Jennifer and Kenneth to react in a completely different manner to the same exact event.

Table 1.1   Schema Lenses

Event	Schema Lens	Reaction
At age four, Jennifer's son, Jerod, starts to whine for some candy in the grocery store after a long day of shopping.	Other-Centered	"Jerod, I understand why you're upset. What do you want? Okay, I'll buy you the gum. Just please be quiet. Other people hate to hear children whine."
At age four, Kenneth's son, Nick, starts to whine for some candy in the grocery store after a long day of shopping.	Excessive-Control	"Nick, stop this nonsense this second. I won't stand for this kind of behavior. You have no right to be so upset." Kenneth proceeds to spank his son.

There are shortcomings to both parents' reactions. Jennifer unintentionally reinforced the whining: because she gave in, Jerod will more likely misbehave in the future. And Kenneth responded with excessive discipline. Thus, Nick could either become overly submissive or seek revenge in the future. Jennifer and Kenneth's schemas, developed in their own childhoods, dictated those responses. If you'd asked each of them what they *should* have done, they might have come up with a better response. But they didn't do it at the time.

Let's look at another comparison to illustrate how schema lenses work (see table 1.2). Jennifer also believes she must be perfect in everything she does. Since perfection is impossible, she usually ends up disappointed. Kenneth believes that things rarely work out the way they should. Dangers and mishaps lurk everywhere in his eyes.

Table 1.2		Schema Lenses
Event	Schema Lens	Reaction
Kenneth's daughter, Lindsey, at age fifteen is getting ready for her first formal dance.	Distrust	"Just how long has this boy had his driver's license? Does he have any tickets? What kind of car is he driving? I want you home before nine o'clock. Now carry this cell phone and call me the minute you get to the dance. Also, call me just before you leave so that I know exactly when you'll get home. Remember, all boys are after just one thing."
Jennifer's son, Jerod, at age fifteen is getting ready for his first formal dance.	Perfectionist	"Jerod, come here and let me fix that tie; it's crooked. And we need to work on that hair. Now, do you remember what you're supposed to do when you pick her up? Don't forget to say hi to her parents and be sure to talk to them. Don't forget to open the door for her. You look just perfect, honey. Be sure to be a gentleman. Don't do anything to embarrass us. Remember, you're on probation."

Again, Kenneth and Jennifer found themselves channeled into pre-dictable parenting patterns. Kenneth excessively emphasized safety due to his profound distrust, while Jennifer focused on perfection in appearance and behavior. Both carried their focus too far. It would have been better simply to tell their kids to be careful and have a good time.

In Summary

Schemas work like lenses through which you view yourself and the world. These lenses explain why different people react to similar events in astonishingly different ways. Astonishing, unless you know what schema lens is at work. Schema lenses make inexplicable behavior understandable. If you're puzzled by your reactions to a mundane circumstance or if you can't fathom why someone you know sometimes looks "crazy," all you have to do is look for the schema lens operating in the background. Puzzling becomes predictable and crazy looks expected.

Kenneth and Jennifer are not bad parents. They both have some realistic concerns. Most parents have said or done a few of the things they said or did in these examples. Nevertheless, their schemas pushed them to overly rigid reactions. Such rigid reactions have unintended, negative results—often the complete opposite of what the parent intended. The next chapter will explain why parents get the opposite of what they want.

Chapter 2

THE UNEXPECTED
NATURE OF OPPOSITES

The Danger of Going
Too Far with Change

The parenting world is full of contradiction. You can probably think of flower children of the sixties whose children became staunch conservatives. Or children of staunch conservatives who became flaming liberals. How about highly educated, successful parents whose children drop out of high school. Or the children of impoverished parents who succeed against all odds? We have found that parenting extremes of any type easily produce unexpected outcomes.

Parenting styles, all too often, go to extremes. For example, parents can focus excessively on the need for discipline and respect for authority. Other parents think their children must have every new toy or all the latest in designer clothes. Some parents are so concerned about education that they attempt to teach their infants to read. And we're sure you've heard the saying, "You can't love your kids too much." But we'll show you how parents sometimes let love cloud common sense. For example, no loving parents want to see their children hurt. That desire can lead parents to rescue their children from the consequences of their own actions, thereby ruining valuable life lessons.

Our next parent, Debra Valenski, wants a good, well-adjusted child. She very much wants people to think highly of her as a parent. She wants her child to be the one who receives awards and adoration at the end of the school year. Yet, her son, Quinton, constantly gets into trouble at school. His teachers and principal referred him to the school psychologist. We meet Debra now at a school meeting with Quinton's teachers, the principal, and the psychologist.

Debra and Quinton

The three o'clock appointment was usually reserved for meeting with the most difficult parents. No one could predict how long these conferences would take. Yet, principal Pat Hansen realizes that the advantage of having extra time is sometimes overridden by the disadvantage of going directly home after a tense meeting. And she knew that this one was likely to be tense. She could hear teachers and staff getting ready in the conference room. Pat, after dozens of meetings with Mrs. Valenski, assumed she would arrive late. Taking one last sip of soda and grabbing Quinton's file, she joins the others.

Pat sits at the head of the conference table and looks around. Quinton's two teachers and Dr. Chavez, the school psychologist, all have notes in front of them. Pat begins, "We have a few minutes. Let's quickly review our agenda. Why don't we start with the teachers' reports?"

Quinton's fifth grade English teacher sighs. "Well, you all know that Quinton's been having the same troubles since the year began. Nothing has changed. He doesn't do his work, he argues, he annoys other students, and he takes no responsibility for any of his behavior. I've had conferences with his mother; she always tells me the work is too boring for him and that's why he misbehaves."

His other teacher nods in agreement, "I see the same thing in math and science. He's disrespectful, he's out of his seat, and he loses his temper over the smallest things. Just yesterday he pushed his partner in science lab to the floor because he wanted to pour the chemicals in the volcano experiment himself. Every time I've tried to talk to Debra she has some excuse for his behavior. She bristles with defensiveness. I just can't get through to her."

"I've seen Quinton on and off for the past two years," Dr. Chavez chimes in. "He has had a history of behavior problems since starting school. I've talked to his mother over and over. She can't get herself to see that Quinton has a problem. She lets him get away with murder at home. Eventually, she explodes at him when he's gone too far. She seems to have a need to blame the school or anyone she can. The sad thing is that Quinton can be a nice kid sometimes. I've also noticed that after these meetings where she blames the school, she often goes home and yells at Quinton. The next day, understandably, Quinton comes back to school and his behavior is even worse. We need to get her to see that Quinton really needs help. And she has to learn to set better limits for him at home and back us up when we set limits on him at school. I'm just not sure how to get the message across."

"It's three-fifteen," Pat says. "Debra should be here any minute. Let's work hard to show her we all really care about Quinton and aren't trying to gang up on him or her. If we've made any mistake in the past, it's that we haven't paid enough attention to Debra's incredible sensitivity to criticism." The discussion continues until Debra walks in, a full thirty minutes late.

Debra already looks agitated as she yanks the empty chair out from the table to sit down. Without apologizing, she begins, "Okay, so what has Quinton done this time?"

Pat calmly summarizes the concerns of the staff with the most positive spin she can. She concludes, "We all need to work together to help Quinton succeed. Debra, what are your thoughts?"

"Things have never been right for Quinton at this school. I admit he had a few problems his first year. But now you circle like vultures waiting for any excuse to blame him. I know for a fact that other kids get away with a lot more than my son. How come he's always getting in trouble when you don't punish other kids for the same thing?"

"I can assure you that's not true in my class. I treat all the kids the same. As a matter of fact, I bend over backwards to help Quinton keep from getting in trouble," the English teacher retorts.

Dr. Chavez swiftly steps in. "Let's focus on Quinton and how we can solve the problem. Debra, you know your son better than anyone at this table. We need your help."

"You people are the professionals. You're the ones who should know how to deal with Quinton!" Debra's volume increases along with her frustration. "What am I supposed to do? I tell him to behave. I can't follow him to school every day."

Pat intercedes. "No one is asking you to do that, Debra. We wonder if there are any problems at home that might be causing some of Quinton's acting out at school. No one is trying to blame you though. We just want to help."

Angrily, Debra shoves her chair back from the table. "This is an ambush. It's the school's fault and you're trying to blame me. I'm not going to sit here for this abuse."

"Please, Debra, hold on a minute. I know how much you care about your son. I really like him too." Debra remains still in her chair as Dr. Chavez continues, "Quinton's bright, charming, and has a great sense of humor. But, something is getting in his way of succeeding in school. We really do need your help. And I'm not sure why you so easily fall into feeling attacked. What's that about?"

"What do you mean?" Debra asks.

"I have to wonder if you don't have a special connection with Quinton that makes you want to protect him. Debra, I sense so much intensity in your reaction. It's clear you care deeply about him. Am I making any sense?"

Tears well up in Debra's eyes. "Quinton is a special child. You know, he almost died when he was a baby."

"I wasn't aware of that. Tell me more about it."

"Quinton had colic. He was crabby all the time. That's why I didn't rush him to the doctor when he wouldn't stop crying for a couple of days. His face used to turn red from screaming so much. I didn't know how sick he was until I picked him up after a nap and he was burning up. He had a convulsion from the fever as I held him in my arms. Quinton was hospitalized for a week and he almost died. The doctor hinted that I was irresponsible for not bringing him in sooner. He also said that Quinton might suffer permanent brain damage. I'll never forgive myself for that. I can't stand to see him hurt. I feel like I have to protect him."

Principal Pat Hansen offers Debra a tissue. No one speaks. Dr. Chavez breaks the silence, "Thank you for sharing that with us, Debra. That must have been difficult. You may not see the connection right now, but I have to wonder if that experience has something to do with what's happening in school and at home. You want so much for Quinton to do well, and yet we all keep struggling. Telling me about his nearly fatal illness gives me insight into part of what may be going on. Would you be willing to spend a few sessions with me to talk about it?"

When Parents Do Too Much of a Good Thing

Debra's goal was to protect Quinton. She felt profound guilt over having let him down as a baby and vowed to never again let harm come his way. Debra desperately desired to keep him out of trouble. She always took his side when anyone accused him of anything. But parents can harm their kids by giving them too much of a good thing. Debra didn't want Quinton to constantly get into trouble at school. She certainly didn't want him to get into fights and show disrespect. But that's what was happening.

Debra's story illustrates how schemas affect parenting. Debra's dominant schema is Blameless. She had a horrible time accepting blame for herself or her kids. When anything went wrong, she tried to find fault elsewhere. Occasionally, as in the case of her son's brush with death, she blames herself excessively, but her dominate schema is still Blameless. And it caused her to overly protect her son from criticism.

Now, let's revisit Kenneth and show how his Distrust schema creates parenting problems. During childhood, Kenneth learned to believe that life is full of disappointments and dangers. Today, his Distrust schema causes him to worry excessively about his teenage daughter's activities. Yet, up to the age of fifteen, Lindsey has never done anything to warrant his concerns. Lindsey has been a decent student, has followed her father's rules, and is a sought-after baby-sitter in the neighborhood. It's good to have some worry and concern for your kids. We all want our kids to be safe. But Kenneth's worries became an obsession that backfired.

Ten minutes after nine. Kenneth shouts at his wife, "Where is that girl? I knew she was going to get in trouble. You should never have let her go to that party. All kids do at parties nowadays is drink and smoke pot. And there's that new drug— what's it called? You know, the one that boys put in girls' drinks to knock them out and rape them. Lindsey's so naive; she makes the perfect target."

Twelve-year-old Nick looks up from his book. "Dad, give her a break. I'm sure she's not doing anything wrong. She's only ten minutes late."

"Nick, I know you never do anything wrong, thank God, but that sister of yours doesn't have your good sense. She's a disaster waiting to happen." The sound of a car door slamming stops Kenneth's tirade.

As Lindsey opens the door, Kenneth launches his usual inquisition. "Why are you late? I told you to be home at nine sharp, not ten after. Come here, let me smell your breath. Have you been drinking? Is that smoke I smell on your jacket? How many kids were doing drugs this time? Don't deny it; just tell me what went on. And look at the way you're dressed. That sweater is way too tight. You're just asking for trouble."

"Dad, I'm the only fifteen-year-old in the universe who has

to be home by nine on a weekend night. I haven't done anything wrong. All that matters is that I wasn't doing anything wrong. Besides, I can take care of myself. You're just jealous because you don't have fun anymore. All you do is sit around looking for something to be angry about."

"I've told you never talk to me that way. That's it. You're grounded for a month." Kenneth storms out of the room.

Lindsey bursts into tears, "Mom, why does it always turn out like this? I can't be grounded. Next week is the winter dance. We already bought the dress. I told Jason I could go with him and he rented a tuxedo. Can't you talk to Dad?"

"You know he *never* backs down. Once he says something, that's it." Sally's eyes mist in sympathy. "I can't change his mind; he'd just get mad at me. I know he's awfully harsh, but he loves you more than anything, honey. He just worries too much about something bad happening to you."

Lindsey doesn't have any idea why her father is so harsh. And she doesn't know that he actually feels sorry after his outbursts. To her, it seems her father comes from another planet. Lindsey thinks her dad is on a crusade to punish her—even for things she hasn't done.

Kenneth doesn't back down because he believes if he changes his mind, Lindsey will see that as an opportunity to run wild. He spends a lot of time wondering why things go so wrong, and he even suspects he's too hard on his daughter. But Kenneth's so afraid Lindsey will get hurt in a world he knows is full of peril. He wants to show he cares. All he does is make his daughter angry and take away her incentive to follow his rules, since he never really believes she is following them anyway.

"Sally, have you noticed how well Lindsey is taking her grounding this time? Maybe I finally got through to her."

Sally looks up from her magazine. "Yes, I have. And the dance began just a little while ago. I thought she'd be whining and complaining all day. Instead, she seems almost chipper. And I love the fact she's reading so much. Maybe she'll learn to love reading as much as Nick. But, frankly, it doesn't seem like her."

Kenneth and Sally turn as their daughter enters the room. "Good night, Mom, Good night, Dad. I love you both. I guess I'm tired from reading all day. I'm going to finish this chapter and go to sleep."

Lindsey turns toward her room, wanting to skip but forcing herself to walk. She knows she has successfully laid the groundwork for her plan. She'll be damned if she'll miss that dance. She carefully arranges pillows under the covers in case her parents look in. Then she hurriedly puts on makeup, adding more than usual since her dad won't be around to censor her appearance. After throwing on her dress, she hikes it up as she climbs out the window. Jason waits nervously at the corner in his parents' car, not quite believing he agreed to this crazy plan.

As Lindsey gets into the car, Jason whispers, "I can't believe we're doing this. Your dad is going to kill me."

"You don't have to whisper, Jason, he can't hear us. Anyway, I feel great. I'm going to do everything I want tonight. Might as well, my dad thinks I do it all anyway." Lindsey leans over giving Jason an uncharacteristically passionate kiss on the lips. Jason feels apprehensive and excited at the same time. He turns up the radio, shifts into first gear, and peels away from the curb.

Soon after arriving at the dance, Jason realizes Lindsey is going to be a handful. He knows she doesn't drink or smoke pot. But tonight she slips out of the dance with a wild group of kids. He leaves the dance to find her outside, it's obvious what they're doing. "Lindsey, what's going on? You don't do this stuff. Come back inside."

Lindsey's speech is already slurred. Jason realizes she must have somehow started drinking earlier. "Oh, Jase, you're *so* straight. Come on and have fun with us. I don't have a curfew and this is *my* night." She throws her arms around his neck and tries to pull him into the group.

"Lindsey, please come inside with me," Jason pleads.

"No way, Mr. Straight. I'm having fun tonight."

"Okay, Lindsey, you're on your own. Let me know if you need a ride."

Lindsey backs away from Jason and turns to the nearest available guy, Michael. Leaning into Michael, she murmurs, "Michael, you'll party with me, won't you? Can you drive me home later? Like, much later."

Michael takes a big swig out of his beer. "Dump the nerd. Let's have a good time." He pulls Lindsey close and hands her a beer.

Jason feels responsible, but he doesn't know what to do. He wanders around the dance for a while and decides to go home. He feels like he shouldn't leave her with these guys, but she made herself clear when she told him to get lost. He hopes she'll be okay. His chest feels tight with anxiety and heavy with a mixture of guilt, hurt, and anger.

The eleven o'clock news concludes. The sound of the telephone startles Kenneth. "Hello."

"Is this Mr. Wieder?"

"Yes, who's this?"

"Ah, Mr. Wieder, this is Officer Hardgrove at the fifth precinct. I'm sorry to disturb you, sir, but it's about your daughter, Lindsey."

"What about my daughter, Lindsey? And just what business do the police have with my daughter? Why the hell are you calling at this hour?"

Officer Hardgrove's voice becomes firmer in response to Kenneth's provocative tone, "Sir, there's been an accident and I'm afraid your daughter was a passenger."

"That's impossible! She's right here in bed." Kenneth shouts to his wife, "Sally, go get Lindsey out of bed. This idiot cop thinks Lindsey's been in an accident."

Sally rushes to her room and discovers the planted pillows and the partly opened window. She turns gray and gasps to Kenneth, "You bastard, you finally did it. We've lost our daughter and it's your fault!"

Fortunately, the accident was minor and Lindsey was not seriously injured. However, all four teens in the car had been drinking and were charged with illegal possession of alcohol by a minor. Strangely enough, when Kenneth arrived at the police station, he broke down sobbing. He finally realized his approach with Lindsey wasn't getting what he wanted. He only wanted to protect her, yet he was driving her into reckless rebellion.

We don't mean to give you the idea that Kenneth was the sole cause of Lindsey's misbehavior. Not by any means. Parents *never* bear the total responsibility for their children's actions, good or bad. School, peers, culture, television, genetics, and a multitude of other influences go into making them who they are. And, at a certain point, the children themselves bear a significant portion of the responsibility for their own actions. At the same time, Kenneth's parenting warranted a significant tune-up. And he finally was starting to see it. When Sally suggested family counseling, he readily agreed.

By contrast, Jennifer, the mother from juvenile court, had already been to a handful of counselors. Most of them gave similar suggestions. Jennifer needed to learn how to say no to her son. Repeatedly, she found herself unable to carry out their advice. None of the counselors explored *why* she found it so difficult to set limits. They hinted that she *actually wanted* Jerod to have problems. But that wasn't the case at all. Her schemas made it virtually impossible for her to apply the counselors' suggestions. Here's how Jennifer's schemas interfered with her parenting some years before the court appearance.

"Daddy lets me stay up 'til ten. It's not fair," whines four-year-old Jerod. Just a year after the divorce and Jerod has already learned to manipulate both of his parents. The counselor's voice rang through Jennifer's head, "You mustn't give into him. Children of divorce often play one side against the other to get what they want."

So Jennifer tells Jerod, "No, sweetie, I don't care what your father does. At this house, you have to go to bed by nine."

"You're mean. Daddy's nice. And he let's me play Nintendo as much as I want. I want to go back to Daddy's house. I don't like you!"

"Oh honey, you don't mean that."

"I do too. I hate you, I hate you, I hate you! I don't want to go to bed. I want to watch TV," Jerod screams.

"I know you don't want to go to bed precious, but it's for your own good. You'll be so tired and you have preschool tomorrow," Jennifer pleads.

Jerod falls to the floor, kicking his feet. "I don't care. I won't be tired. I wanna go to Daddy's. I wanna go to Daddy's. I wanna go to Daddy's."

"All right, just for tonight, sweetie. Give momma a kiss."

Jerod instantly transforms, calmly saying, "Thanks, Mommy. I love you."

Jennifer knew then, as she had so many other times, that her response wasn't the right thing to do. While Jennifer tried to give Jerod everything he *wanted*, she ended up not giving him what he *needed*. Too much of a good thing turned sour. Why couldn't she follow the advice she'd been given?

As we said before, Jennifer has the Other-Centered and Anxious-Attachment schemas. She believes the people she cares about will either leave or become emotionally unavailable. Jennifer usually puts other people's needs before her own. So, Jennifer would go out of her way to do things for Jerod. If Other-Centered had been the only schema operating, she might have been able to resist her son. However, Jerod also managed to trigger her Anxious-Attachment schema when he told her he hated her and wanted to go to his dad's house. At that point, her ability to reason vanished and anxious emotions overwhelmed her.

The truth is, no four-year-old child is going to stop loving a parent over any reasonable degree of limit setting. And Jerod certainly won't stop loving Jennifer if she sends him to bed. But her Anxious-Attachment prevented her from seeing this fairly obvious reality. Or perhaps we should say the reality is obvious to someone who doesn't have this schema, but not so obvious to someone who does. The lens of her Anxious-Attachment schema clouded Jennifer's vision of reality.

The Unexpected Nature of Opposites

Years later, Jennifer gave up custody of Jerod to a juvenile judge. She completely abandoned him and walked right out of the courtroom. Now, wait a minute. Jennifer has an Anxious-Attachment schema, meaning she desperately feared losing anyone she cared about. Yet she gave up her own son. How can you reconcile that puzzling contradiction? Jennifer went from wanting Jerod incredibly close to her to the opposite—wanting nothing to do with him. In other words, Jennifer actually flipped from an Anxious-Attachment schema to the opposite schema of Avoidant-Attachment. In order to understand *why* someone would do that, we have to explain a little about the nature of opposites.

Schemas, like almost everything else, consist of a pair of opposites. Opposites provide meaning to concepts and perceptions. If you think about it, how would you know what the concept of *long* means without knowing its opposite, *short*? Or how would you understand *hot* without knowing what *cold* is?

Every schema also has an opposite. We've already introduced you to a variety of schemas. The full list of schema pairs is shown in the following table. We'll define them more fully in chapter 3.

Problematic Parenting Schemas	
Anxious-Attachment (afraid of losing others)	Avoidant-Attachment (avoids intimacy and closeness)
Blameworthy (guilt is my middle name)	Blameless (assumes no responsibility, blames others)
Naive (everything will work out)	Distrust (the world is out to get me)

Other-Centered (others' needs take center stage)	Self-Centered (me, me, me)
Perfectionist (excessive standards)	Unambitious (lack of standards)
No Play (joyless, all work)	All Play (party animal)
Excessive-Control (disciplinarian)	No Control (anything goes)

But are schema opposites such as these truly at opposite ends of the spectrum? In Eastern philosophy, yin and yang are opposites. Yin refers to the feminine side of your personality. Yin is intuitive, complex, submissive, and receptive. Yang, the masculine side, is rational, simple, dominant, and directive. Each of these opposites produces the other. Thus, yin and the yang are always depicted as containing the seeds of their own opposites at the extreme. The idea is that one side never dominates forever, so all things eventually change into their opposites. As you can see in Figure 2.1, yin and yang swirl into each other.

Ying/yang theory demonstrates how the more opposite two things appear, the more they become the same. For example, the opposite of infancy is extreme old age. Both have striking similarities such as dependency, less control over bodily functions, and reduced thinking ability as compared to the middle stage of adulthood. Like extreme heat, extreme cold, such as dry ice, burns the flesh. And violet and red, though they are the most opposite on the

Figure 2.1

color wavelength spectrum, appear far more similar to the eye than green which lies in the middle.

Because extreme opposites share more in common with each other than they do with the middle ground, parents can harm their kids by giving them too much of a good thing. Too much good easily turns into bad. You can show too much love and it turns into spoiling. Too much discipline can produce rebellion. Too much overprotection can produce children unable to defend themselves.

Each schema appears to have an opposite schema. In some sense they are opposite. And yet they have many striking similarities. Schemas at their opposite extremes share five critical characteristics:

- *Schemas lead to extreme moods.* Either side of a schema pair leads to intense emotions in response to events. Jennifer, the mother of Jerod, has a Perfectionist schema. You might remember the terror she experienced prior to performing on the piano for her parents' guests. Today, whenever she makes the smallest mistake, she feels horribly depressed and inadequate. Similarly, Kenneth's Distrust schema causes him to feel overly fearful whenever his daughter leaves the house. These intense emotions occur over and over again in Jennifer and Kenneth. Studies have shown that chronic, intense emotions can cause high blood pressure, heart disease, and other health problems.

- *Schemas disregard contradictory evidence.* Teachers had told Debra about Quinton's problems at school since the first grade. Different people gave her the message at different times and in different ways. Mounds of evidence supported the fact that Quinton had a behavior problem. But Debra couldn't allow herself to hear it. She always found an excuse; it was either the teacher's fault, another kid, or poor school curriculum that supposedly bored her son. Her schema would not let the truth in. It worked like an umbrella that kept the rain of criticism away.

- *Schemas put stress on relationships.* Kenneth and his wife Sally argued for years over his paranoid vigilance concerning his children. When his Distrust schema caused him to impose absurd curfews, dress standards, and rules, Sally tried in vain to reason with him. Fight after fight took place over this issue. Productive discussion was nowhere in sight. Making matters worse, Kenneth had an Excessive-Control schema that prevented him from giving in on anything: he had to take charge, and he alone knew what was best for his family. Sally had almost given up on the idea of getting through to him until their daughter's escapade created a crisis.

- *Schemas create negative outcomes in children.* All children need guidance and limits set for them by their parents. They don't need their desires met at every moment. But Jennifer could not say no to her son. Without appropriate limits, her son predictably went out of control. The result: Jerod found limits imposed by the juvenile justice system. Kenneth's daughter, Lindsey, also needed guidance and limits. However, Kenneth gave her all too much of these. Lindsey ultimately rebelled from the unrelenting guidance and limits. And Debra, by constantly excusing her son's actions, gave him no incentive or motivation to succeed in school. Sadly, they are all well-intentioned and loving parents, yet their children suffered. Parenting gone awry, due to schemas lurking in the background.
- *Opposite schemas are rigid.* The more extreme a schema, the more rigid it becomes. Schemas usually develop over many years. They become an ingrained part of your personality. They don't change easily. Debra, the mother who accused the school of being too hard on her son, had a Blameless schema rooted in her childhood. When little Debra misbehaved, her mother made up excuses for her. Little Debra could do no wrong in her mother's eyes. Now as a mother, Debra carries out the tradition with her son, Quinton. Debra doesn't take responsibility for herself, nor does she assign responsibility to her kid. At least usually. But sometimes she does just the opposite. When she does, watch out. She either pummels herself or her kid unmercifully. Which takes us to our next point.

Schema Flipping

Because a schema's opposite actually has as many similarities as differences, it's easier to flip between opposites than find the middle ground. That's what happened to Jennifer when she walked out of the courtroom, giving up custody of Jerod. Jennifer had spent so many years focused on his needs and trying to hold on to his love, she burned out. She couldn't take the emotional pain. Her only way of dealing with the pain was to avoid it completely by flipping from Anxious-Attachment to Avoidant-Attachment. She went from total immersion with Jerod to total abandonment, having no clue there might be a better way. Let's take a look at what happened after Jennifer walked out of the courtroom.

Jennifer brushes the tears away as she climbs into her car at the courthouse parking lot. She cranks the volume up on the radio, rolls the window down, and speeds off to work. By the time she arrives, she's more composed. She walks quickly past the receptionist, nodding a quick hello. At her desk, she turns on the computer and starts to work.

"Jennifer, what happened in court?" her friend inquires.

"I did just what I said I would. I did everything I could for him. He's no longer my son."

"How are you feeling about this? It must be awfully hard to do what you did."

"I feel terrible. I was so tired taking care of him. He turned out just like his father," Jennifer replied, struggling to hold on to her decision. She picks up her ringing phone, anxious to focus on her work and put Jerod out of her mind.

"Hello, Mrs. Dearborn, this is Trevor Wolfe, your son's probation officer. Um . . . I saw what happened at court today. I wanted to let you know that I support you entirely, but Jerod doesn't really belong in the juvenile detention center. He has problems, Mrs. Dearborn, but you have no idea how much more troubled most of the kids in the center really are. Your son has potential. We can get more therapy and I can work with him more closely. We just don't have to go this far. The judge has agreed to release him to your custody. Let us work with you."

"I guess no one really heard me in court today. I meant what I said. I've been through this too many times. I've tried everything I know how to do. You don't understand how hard it's been." Jennifer starts crying.

"But, Mrs. Dearborn, Jerod isn't really a bad boy. Yes, he was arrested once before, but it was a minor charge and so is this one. Kids like this often turn out okay if we just work together. Frankly, I'm surprised at your attitude."

"Mr. Wolfe, you aren't listening to me. I gave Jerod my whole life. There was nothing I wouldn't do for him. I can't do any more. I just can't." Jennifer hangs up the phone.

We aren't saying that so-called tough love isn't a good idea sometimes. But Jerod was blindsided. His mother had always been there for him. She had done everything she could. She'd done too much. And she hadn't set the needed limits. If she could have, it might have worked. But her extreme overindulgence of her son had finally created a crescendo of hopelessness in her. By totally walking away, she wasn't giving him tough love, she was abandoning her responsibility. She had flipped schema from Anxious-Attachment to Avoidant-Attachment.

To understand such flipping, it might be useful to think of schema pairs as lying on a continuum, like a ruler that goes from one end to the other. But unlike a ruler, schema continuums are not straight lines. They wrap back onto themselves as depicted in figure 2.2. As you can see, the extreme ends approach each other.

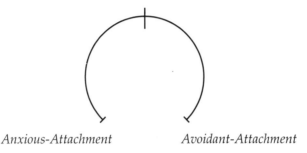

Anxious-Attachment   *Avoidant-Attachment*

Figure 2.2

Notice how the opposite schemas lie closer to each other than they do to the middle of the continuum. That's because of their great similarity. Both are rigid, produce extreme moods, disregard contradictory evidence, put stress on relationships, and create negative outcomes in children.

Let's look at another example of schema flipping. Debra has a Blameless schema—nothing is her fault. Thus, she vigilantly looks out for possible criticism and blame in order to prepare her defenses and ward them off. Most of the time her defenses work. Now, we'll take a look at Debra in the hospital back when Quinton was an infant. This time her defenses failed. Debra flipped from Blameless to Blameworthy.

"Mrs. Valenski, your son is seriously ill. I believe he must have been sick for at least several days. Did you see any symptoms in the last few days?" Dr. Brownell inquired.

"Doctor, he has colic; he's always crying. Maybe he cried a little more in the last few days. And his face was flushed, but I just thought that was because he was crying so much. Of course, I was out last night, and that damn baby-sitter should have told me he looked this bad. That's the last time I'll use her."

"Well, we have the fever down now, but it was too high for too long; that's why he had the convulsions. I don't think he'll have any brain damage, but we'll have to watch his fevers a little more closely in the future, okay?"

"Brain damage? What are you talking about?"

"Mrs. Valenski, occasionally children who have had convulsions and high fevers sustain damage to their brains. You never can tell."

"God. Not my son. It's all my fault. I should never have gone out last night. I'll never forgive myself. Oh, what if he's a vegetable? I'm not fit to be a mother." Debra's voice rises hysterically, "God, how could I be so stupid?"

"Oh, Mrs. Valenski, please calm down, I wasn't implying that. I'm not saying anything about your mothering. And it's very unlikely that he'll suffer any permanent brain damage. He's certainly not going to be a vegetable. You're overreacting. You just need to be careful with fevers in an infant, that's all."

Debra's schema kept her on the lookout for any possible signs of criticism. Often she saw denigration of herself when none was intended. So, when the doctor merely asked if she'd seen any signs of illness, she interpreted the question as an attack. She immediately blamed the baby-sitter. Then, when he suggested the possibility of brain damage, her defenses broke down. She overreacted with a barrage of self-criticism. She flipped from Blameless to Blameworthy. She couldn't see there was a middle ground. In this case, the middle ground would have consisted of her acknowledging the need for greater attentiveness to fevers, but without excessive self-flagellation. There is something called a Middle Way. Below we show you where it lies on the schema continuum.

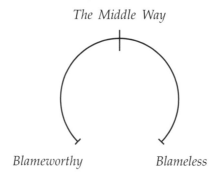

The Middle Way

Blameworthy   *Blameless*

Figure 2.3

Buddhism has contended for centuries that the path to enlightenment is the Middle Way, or the line between all opposite extremes. But the

Middle Way is often surprisingly elusive. Imagine yourself positioned at the extreme end of either the Blameworthy or the Blameless pole. The Middle Way lies out of your field of vision and the path toward it is steep and precipitous. In the following chapters we will help you learn to find the Middle Way whenever you're engulfed in parenting chaos created by your schemas.

In Summary

We talked about how opposites often become more alike than different, especially at the extremes. This principle applies to schemas. That's why it's so easy to flip between schema opposites. And both schema extremes causes problems for parents and children.

The path out of chaos leads you toward the Middle Way, which can calm your parenting, your kids, and your life. We'll help you navigate the path, but you'll probably get lost at times. We'll help you learn to get back on the path. Sometimes you'll find the trail strewn with obstacles and unexpected traps. Don't be discouraged; the rewards are more than worth the effort. You can start being the parent you always wanted to be. The Middle Way will calm chaos and allow you to parent like you want.

Parenting Practice

Let's examine whether or not you've ever flipped from one schema extreme to another, or if you've ever felt the urge to do so. The first example is of opposite schemas related to the issue of parental control. A parent with an Excessive Control schema is an overly strict disciplinarian, often fearing disaster if rules aren't enforced vigorously at all times. On the other hand, a parent with a No Control schema has a hard time enforcing rules and limits. Most parents fall somewhere in between, but you're also likely to go a little too far in one direction or another. And if you do, you might find yourself flipping to the opposite extreme rather than moving to the Middle Way. Here's what we mean.

Have you ever let your children get away with things for a little too long? For example, perhaps you let them watch too much TV. Or, maybe you were too tired to make them do their homework or household chores. It is hard to find the right balance on such things. But, later, if you've gone too far in the direction of No Control, you may eventually get resentful. One night, seeing your kids spaced out, staring mindlessly at the TV, surrounded by half-empty soda cans and junk food bags, you flip. Suddenly, you fly into a rage, declare

TV off-limits, and scream at them to pick up. This "flip" to Excessive Control, may make you feel tempted to go further and further, leading you to go from having no limits to banning television from the house forever or setting other unreasonable limits.

Now, try to go through your memory and see if you can recall any similar incidents with your children and your parenting. It is important to understand that schema flipping can go in both directions. For example, an Excessive-Control parent might tire of the battles and announce to the child, "I don't care what you do anymore."

In the following chart, write down examples from your parenting experiences. If you can't think of an instance when you flipped from one end to the other, maybe your memories of your own parents' actions toward you will provide an example.

Schema Flipping	
Example of when you fell into Excessive-Control	Examples of when you fell into No Control

The second example looks at opposite schemas related to the issue of standards. Parents with a perfectionist schema feel there's a right way and a wrong way to do things with little in between. A child's work, grades, or performances are either perfect or worthless. By contrast, parents with an unambitious schema care little about such matters. Getting by is good enough for them, and they don't ask much of their kids in this area. Again, most parents fall somewhere in between. But, you're also likely to go a little too far in one direction or the other. And if you do, you might find yourself flipping too far in the other direction.

Have you ever gotten overly involved in one of your kid's science projects? Possibly to the extent that you stayed up late and ended up doing more work on it than your child? Maybe after three or four years of you winning grade school science awards instead of your kid, you finally get fed up. When your child comes to you with a project due tomorrow, you throw your hands in the air, declaring, "I'm never giving you help again. Not on science projects, homework, or whatever. And, I don't care what you do or how it comes out. That's it! Enough already!" This is an example of flipping.

In the following chart, write down examples from your parenting experiences. If you can't think of an instance when you flipped from one end to the other, maybe your memories of your own parents during your childhood will provide an example.

Schema Flipping	
Examples of when you became Perfectionist	Examples of when you became Unambitious

Chapter 3

ASSESSING YOUR PARENTING STYLE

What Makes Parenting So Hard

Kenneth clings to his steaming cup of coffee. "I just want you to know, Dr. Douglas, I'm not a believer in this therapy thing. I think people should be able to solve their own problems. I'm not going to sit here talking about my dreams while you nod your head for over a hundred dollars an hour. The only reason I'm here is that Sally insists we do this. And I'm willing to do anything to help Lindsey. Of course, Nick is doing just fine. He's never shown the slightest problem. He doesn't talk back to me and he always makes the honor roll. I just don't know what's gone wrong with Lindsey."

Rocking back in his chair, Dr. Douglas, a clinical psychologist, tries to sound reassuring. "I'm glad to hear you're concerned about your kids. And I'm glad you have healthy skepticism about therapy. We won't spend a whole lot of time on your dreams. And I'll work hard with you to develop some clear ideas about what's going on and what we can do about it. Bear with me this week, Kenneth, because I need to collect a lot of information. Then together we'll set goals and specific ways of getting there."

Dr. Douglas notices Kenneth's finely tailored suit and stiff demeanor, which contrasts with his own, more informal shirt, tie, and jeans. Sally appears more comfortable than her husband, dressed in cotton slacks and a simple knit shirt. Dr. Douglas wonders if their dress reflects their personalities. Kenneth's formality seems to put up a wall; Sally looks more approachable. Dr. Douglas proceeds to obtain background information about the family and review their concerns. Kenneth finds himself caught by surprise when Dr. Douglas turns to him and says, "Kenneth, I realize this may seem off the subject, but I often find it very helpful to know about parents' childhoods. Could you tell me what it was like to grow up in your family?"

"You're right, I think it's off the subject. But I promised Sally I would cooperate with this. And I mean that. I do want to help my kids in any way I can. What exactly do you want to know?" Kenneth straightens up in his chair. "My family was just like anyone else's."

"I'm not trying to say there was anything abnormal about your family. How about we start with how many brothers and sisters you had?"

"Okay, I had one older brother."

"How did you two get along?"

"Like any two brothers I suppose. We had our ups and downs. I don't see much of him anymore. I doubt he has anything to do with Lindsey's problems."

"I know this seems really off the point, Kenneth, but sometimes it's surprising how much we can learn from an overview like this. Try to bear with me, okay?"

"Sure." Kenneth shrugs.

"For instance, tell me about holidays in your family."

"Our holidays were like any other family's, I guess."

"Does any holiday stand out to you?"

Kenneth thinks for a moment, then replies, "Well, it's pretty stupid, but there was one Christmas. I repeatedly had been promised a train set. God, I wanted that train. Stupid, really. But my dad gave me an encyclopedia instead. Really, that was a more practical present for a kid, but I was so disappointed."

"Whether it was a better present or not, Kenneth, how did it make you feel when you opened up the package and found an encyclopedia?"

Kenneth blinks with surprise at the unexpected tears welling in his eyes. "Gosh, I hadn't thought about that for years. I guess I was devastated. He promised that train. Yeah, I was really disappointed."

"Tell me about other times you felt that kind of let down, Kenneth."

"You know, my dad and brother were always trying to trick me. They would promise me things and laugh when I took the bait. I was a born sucker. It was probably good training. I learned to distrust everything and everyone. Maybe that's why I'm such a good corporate attorney."

"You know, those experiences probably did teach you some useful things, Kenneth. And perhaps they have given you trouble as well. I think now would be a good time to introduce you to a new concept that explains a lot about why we feel and react to things the way we do. Would that be all right?"

"Sure. I just hope it isn't a bunch of meaningless psychobabble mumbo jumbo," Kenneth sighs.

"If it seems that way, let me know." Dr. Douglas continues, "You know that different people often look at the very same event in quite different ways. For example, from what you both said, when Lindsey is a few minutes late coming home, Sally doesn't get too concerned. You, on the other hand, immediately start to worry that something awful has happened. In reality, neither of you truly know why Lindsey is late, but you have very different assumptions about what has happened. Why?"

Sally responds, "I guess I just trust her more. I think it might be that ..."

Kenneth cuts her off, his voice rising, "God, Sally, you're out to lunch about today's kids. Have you forgotten what she did at that dance?"

Dr. Douglas makes a time-out motion with his hands. "Hold on. You both actually have a point here. And it's perfectly understandable why you see things in different ways. That's exactly what I'm getting at. Let me tell you about the way our brains form meaning about things. A term called 'schemas' describes the way we all learn to look at things. I know the word sounds like psychobabble, Kenneth, but let me tell you more about it."

Kenneth asks, "Isn't that like a schematic drawing that provides you with an outline, a plan, or overview of something?"

"That's quite right, Kenneth. But rather than schematic drawings, schemas involve an organized way of thinking about ourselves and the world. In a sense they're like strongly held beliefs, yet they do more than mere beliefs. For instance, Kenneth, during your childhood, the rug was pulled out from under you all the time. So you learned to distrust the world. Anyone with a childhood like yours would likely have formed a Distrust schema. Now, when anything happens that presents the remotest chance of danger, your Distrust schema kicks in, setting off a piercing alarm that you find impossible to ignore. That's why you worry so much about your kids. Sally, on the other hand, grew up in a family that followed through on their promises more often than yours did. She didn't learn to worry as much as you do."

"Oh, I get it. This is blame-Kenneth time. It's a setup. Sally brings me to therapy to help our family and I become the scapegoat for all our problems."

"Kenneth, this isn't about blame. I really want you to hear me on this. Sally has schemas that get in the way of her being the parent she'd like to be, too. No one asks to have the schemas they have. We come by them honestly. They make perfect sense during childhood when most of them are formed. It's just that when we're adults, the world is quite different than when we were kids. Yet we still look at the world through the same schemas. Schemas act like a lens that we look at the world through. The trouble is, we need to update the prescription, but we may not do it until we identify our schemas and realize we're looking through distorted lenses."

At the conclusion of his discussion, Dr. Douglas says, "Now that you understand about schemas, we need to take a closer look at which schemas interfere with the way both of you parent. I have a questionnaire for the two of you to fill out by our next session. Does that sound like something you could do?"

Feeling a bit less defensive, Kenneth answers, "Why not? I guess it could be interesting. It can't hurt."

Sally, relieved to hear Kenneth's response, thanks the doctor as they leave. She stuffs her questionnaire into her overflowing purse.

Assessing Your Problematic Parenting Schemas

The process of change starts by discovering exactly what you need to change. In other words, *awareness*. If you don't know what the problem is, how are you going to do anything about it? Below we present you with our *Parenting Schema Questionnaire*. Try to answer frankly, not the way you think you *should*. Of course, you might think you know what the "right" answer is. If you answer that way, you will not help yourself. Sometimes it's painful to acknowledge problems, but if you can open yourself up to seeing them, real change becomes possible.

When you review the descriptions, please examine each one carefully. At first, you might believe a particular description doesn't apply to you at all. Before you mark your response, consider how you feel—not just how you *think* (for example, how do you feel and react when either your partner or your child criticizes you? Do you tighten up, does your face flush, and/or do you immediately deny the criticism without stopping to think about whether it might be partially true?). Take enough time with each description to both think and feel it through until you are sure whether and to what extent it may apply to you.

Even though the descriptions appear as opposite pairs, you may discover that neither apply to you or just one does. And sometimes you might discover that *both* pairs apply to you often. Don't worry. As we discussed in chapter 2, flipping between opposites is not uncommon.

We also suggest you consider asking your partner or a trusted friend to fill out this questionnaire based on his or her perception of you. We've provided an extra form for that purpose. The reason this is a good idea is that sometimes others can see things in you that you might miss. It's a good idea to compare your responses with someone else's evaluation of you. However, only do this with someone you feel comfortable with and who knows you and your parenting very well. Encourage this person to be as honest as possible about his or her perception. Don't ask anyone you're having a conflict or relationship problem with. This will only fuel the fire.

PARENTING SCHEMA QUESTIONNAIRE

Directions: If any part of the statement strongly applies to you, underline it and consider just that part, ignoring the parts that do not apply. After reading the description in each box, record the number (0–4) that best describes your beliefs and feelings.

0	1	2	3	4
Almost Never Describes Me	Occasionally Describes Me	Sometimes Describes Me	Usually Describes Me	Almost Always Describes Me

____ I often worry about whether my child loves and likes me. I also worry about whether I could go on if anything happened to my child.	____ I believe kids are to be seen and not heard. I am uncomfortable with hugging and kissing. I don't feel my child needs to hear "I love you." I don't spend a lot of time with my kid.

_____ I never feel like I do a good job of parenting. If something goes wrong, I feel like it's all my fault. When my kid gets in trouble, I feel like it's all my fault.	_____ I hate admitting I made a mistake. When someone blames me for something, I usually find someone or something else to blame. When my kid gets into trouble, it's usually someone else's fault, certainly not mine.
_____ I never worry about my kid getting hurt or into trouble. Everything always works out for the best. There's no reason not to trust people. I trust my child completely.	_____ I am a worrywart. The world is a dangerous place. People are out to get you. I can't easily trust my kid. Even if I could trust my own kid, other kids are likely to get him or her into trouble.
_____ I can't do enough for my kid. My kid's needs are far more important than my own.	_____ My needs come first. Raising my child often feels like an intrusion in my life.
_____ I think if something is worth doing, it is worth doing perfectly. There is a right way and a wrong way to do things. I expect my child to hold to the same high standards I have for myself.	_____ I don't worry at all about how well my kid does at school or anything else. As long as my kid gets by, that's good enough for me. It's stupid to put more effort into something than you have to.
_____ Life is serious. Play is a frivolous waste of time. My child's worth will come from work.	_____ The focus for my family is on having a good time. We play as much as we can. We only work to get the absolute essentials done. Life is meant for fun.
_____ Nothing is more important than having strict discipline. Otherwise, a family would be utter chaos. My kid toes the line or else.	_____ I can't say no to my kid. When I do make rules, I have a very hard time enforcing them, especially when my kid gets upset.

PARENTING SCHEMA QUESTIONNAIRE

(To be filled out by a partner or trusted friend)

Directions: If any part of the statement strongly applies to the parent in question, underline it and consider just that part, ignoring the parts that do not apply. After reading the description in each box, record the number (0–4) that you would choose if you were the parent in question.

0	1	2	3	4
Almost Never Describes Me	Occasionally Describes Me	Sometimes Describes Me	Usually Describes Me	Almost Always Describes Me

____ I often worry about whether my child loves and likes me. I also worry about whether I could go on if anything happened to my child.	____ I believe kids are to be seen and not heard. I am uncomfortable with hugging and kissing. I don't feel my child needs to hear "I love you." I don't spend a lot of time with my kid.
____ I never feel like I do a good job of parenting. If something goes wrong, I feel like it's all my fault. When my kid gets in trouble, I feel like it's all my fault.	____ I hate admitting I made a mistake. When someone blames me for something, I usually find someone or something else to blame. When my kid gets into trouble, it's usually someone else's fault, certainly not mine.
____ I never worry about my kid getting hurt or into trouble. Everything always works out for the best. There's no reason not to trust people. I trust my child completely.	____ I am a worrywart. The world is a dangerous place. People are out to get you. I can't easily trust my kid. Even if I could trust my own kid, other kids are likely to get him or her into trouble.
____ I can't do enough for my kid. My kid's needs are far more important than my own.	____ My needs come first. Raising my child often feels like an intrusion in my life.

____ I think if something is worth doing, it is worth doing perfectly. There is a right way and a wrong way to do things. I expect my child to hold to the same high standards I have for myself.	____ I don't worry at all about how well my kid does at school or anything else. As long as my kid gets by, that's good enough for me. It's stupid to put more effort into something than you have to.
____ Life is serious. Play is a frivolous waste of time. My child's worth will come from work.	____ The focus for my family is on having a good time. We play as much as we can. We only work to get the absolute essentials done. Life is meant for fun.
____ Nothing is more important than having strict discipline. Otherwise, a family would be utter chaos. My kid toes the line or else.	____ I can't say no to my kid. When I do make rules, I have a very hard time enforcing them, especially when my kid gets upset.

PARENTING SCHEMA QUESTIONNAIRE

Directions: Now take the scores you and your partner or friend gave yourself for the descriptions on the previous page. Record in the same order below. This will allow you to see which schemas correspond with which statements.

__2__ **Anxious-Attachment:** I often worry about whether my child loves and likes me. I also worry about whether I could go on if anything happened to my child.	__0__ **Avoidant-Attachment:** I believe kids are to be seen and not heard. I am uncomfortable with hugging and kissing. I don't feel my child needs to hear "I love you." I don't spend a lot of time with my kid.

_0_ **Blameworthy:** I never feel like I do a good job of parenting. If something goes wrong, I feel like it's all my fault. When my kid gets in trouble, I feel like it's all my fault.

_1_ **Blameless:** I hate admitting I made a mistake. When someone blames me for something, I usually find someone or something else to blame. When my kid gets into trouble, it's usually someone else's fault, certainly not mine.

_2_ **Naive:** I never worry about my kid getting hurt or getting into trouble. Everything always works out for the best. There's no reason not to trust people. I trust my child completely.

_1_ **Distrust:** I am a worry-wart. The world is a dangerous place. People are out to get you. I can't easily trust my kid. Even if I could trust my own kid, other kids are likely to get him or her into trouble.

_2_ **Other-Centered:** I can't do enough for my kid. My kid's needs are far more important than my own.

_2_ **Self-Centered:** My needs come first. Raising my child often feels like an intrusion in my life.

_3_ **Perfectionist:** I think if something is worth doing, it is worth doing perfectly. There is a right way and a wrong way to do things. I expect my child to hold to the same high standards I have for myself.

_6_ **Unambitious:** I don't worry at all about how well my kid does at school or anything else. As long as my kid gets by, that's good enough for me. It's stupid to put more effort into something than you have to.

_2_ **No Play:** Life is serious. Play is a frivolous waste of time. My child's worth will come from work.

_1_ **All Play:** The focus for my family is on having a good time. We play as much as we can. We only work to get the absolute essentials done. Life is meant for fun.

_2_ **Excessive-Control**: Nothing is more important than having strict discipline. Otherwise, a family would be utter chaos. My kid toes the line or else.	_0_ **No Control**: I can't say no to my kid. When I do make rules, I have a very hard time enforcing them, especially when my kid gets upset.

Now that you've completed the exercise, look over your scores. Any item or part of an item that you recorded as two or above might present a problem for your parenting, at least occasionally. However, we will focus our attention on the obviously problematic schemas that you rated as three or four. It is possible some of the items you rated as two cause more trouble than you think. Perhaps it would help if you checked with your partner or a close friend.

Don't panic if you gave yourself a large number of threes and fours. We'll show you how to deal with them. Realize you acquired those problematic schemas through no fault of your own. Now that you're starting to know your problematic parenting schemas, it will also be important to understand how they undermine your parenting efforts. We rejoin Kenneth and Sally in their next therapy session.

In Dr. Douglas' waiting room, Sally pulls the crumpled questionnaires from the disarray of her purse. Kenneth sighs in disgust, "My God, those questionnaires have melted chocolate all over them. How can we take those into Dr. Douglas? He's going to think we're pigs."

"Lighten up, Kenneth, who cares what he thinks? This is exactly what's wrong with you, you're so uptight about everything having to be perfect."

Dr. Douglas calls the couple into his office. After preliminary greetings and ascertaining no crises needing urgent attention, he inquires, "So, I see you remembered to fill out the Parenting Schema Questionnaires. Could I take a look at what you came up with?"

"Excuse my wife, Dr. Douglas. I'm afraid she isn't very careful with things. That's chocolate on those questionnaires. Her purse is like a dumpster."

"Well, I can deal with a little chocolate. For right now, let's just take a look at what you guys came up with."

KENNETH'S PARENTING SCHEMA QUESTIONNAIRE

0	1	2	3	4
Almost Never Describes Me	Occasionally Describes Me	Sometimes Describes Me	Usually Describes Me	Almost Always Describes Me

__0__ **Anxious-Attachment:** I often worry about whether my child loves and likes me. I also worry about whether I could go on if anything happened to my child.

__2__ **Avoidant-Attachment:** I believe kids are to be seen and not heard. I am uncomfortable with hugging and kissing. I don't feel my child needs to hear "I love you." I don't spend a lot of time with my kid.

__1__ **Blameworthy:** I never feel like I do a good job of parenting. If something goes wrong, I feel like it's all my fault. When my kid gets in trouble, I feel like it's all my fault.

__1__ **Blameless:** I hate admitting I made a mistake. When someone blames me for something, I usually find someone or something else to blame. When my kid gets into trouble, it's usually someone else's fault, certainly not mine.

__1__ **Naive:** I never worry about my kid getting hurt or getting into trouble. Everything always works out for the best. There's no reason not to trust people. I trust my child completely.

__4__ **Distrust:** I am a worrywart. The world is a dangerous place. People are out to get you. I can't easily trust my kid. Even if I could trust my own kid, other kids are likely to get him or her into trouble.

__1__ **Other-Centered:** I can't do enough for my kid. My kid's needs are far more important than my own.

__2__ **Self-Centered:** My needs come first. Raising my child often feels like an intrusion in my life.

__3_ **Perfectionist:** I think if something is worth doing, it is worth doing perfectly. There is a right way and a wrong way to do things. I expect my child to hold to the same high standards I have for myself.	__0_ **Unambitious:** I don't worry at all about how well my kid does at school or anything else. As long as my kid gets by, that's good enough for me. It's stupid to put more effort into something than you have to.
__3_ **No Play:** Life is serious. Play is a frivolous waste of time. My child's worth will come from work.	__0_ **All Play:** The focus for my family is on having a good time. We play as much as we can. We only work to get the absolute essentials done. Life is meant for fun.
__4_ **Excessive-Control:** Nothing is more important than having strict discipline. Otherwise, a family would be utter chaos. My kid toes the line or else.	__0_ **No Control:** I can't say no to my kid. When I do make rules, I have a very hard time enforcing them, especially when my kid gets upset.

Dr. Douglas reviews Kenneth's form first. "Kenneth, thanks for doing this. Did anything on the form strike you as particularly interesting?"

"I know from what you've told us about schemas that any of these I have marked as a three or four are supposed to be a problem. And I guess I sort of see that, but frankly it doesn't feel that way."

"Well, that's right, Kenneth. Often people don't feel their schemas are problems. That's because your schemas have been with you for so long. They've been with you since childhood. You've never learned to look at things in any other way. The problem is that schemas in the extreme cause trouble in ways we aren't even aware of. So let's take a look at a couple of yours to see how that might be so."

"So my so-called schemas are wrong and Sally's are right?"

"Not at all, Kenneth. *Any* schema that goes to the extreme causes problems. That's all. They aren't right or wrong. They just cause trouble. Remember, we acquire the schemas we have for good reasons. And everyone has a few that are out of balance at one time or another. We'll look at both of your sets of parenting schemas to see where some tune-ups might be in order. So, let's start with your Excessive-Control schema. You gave yourself a four on that one. Tell me what that's about for you."

"Well, Dr. Douglas, I can't imagine what would happen if we let our kids run wild. Look at the world today. I recently read where a couple of boys under the age of ten actually sexually assaulted and murdered a thirteen-year-old girl. That's what happens when you don't discipline your kids."

"Actually, Kenneth, a total lack of discipline can cause a lot of problems. I would venture to guess that those kids had other troubles in their lives beyond a lack of discipline, but you do have a good point. The problem is that when we fear one outcome, it often causes us to overreact. Discipline clearly is a good thing for kids. No doubt about it. Unfortunately, when you give too much of it, you can easily end up getting the opposite of what you hope for. Often we find that excessive discipline actually creates resentment and anger. Over time, resentment and anger set the stage for acting out and rebellion. In Lindsey's case, after her escapade, she told you both that she did it because she felt suffocated and constantly accused of things she hadn't done. She was angry about missing the dance. She figured she had nothing to lose because she's grounded so much of the time anyway. And she said that Kenneth thought she was a tramp, so she might as well act like one. Now I realize that Lindsey was absolutely wrong to do what she did. But it appears you didn't get what you wanted out of your discipline. Does this make any sense to you, Kenneth?"

"Well, okay, sure. I do sometimes feel pretty awful when I overreact and give a consequence way out of proportion to the crime. I don't know what happens; the words fall out of my mouth. Then I can't back down. But I guess I can see it isn't getting me what I want."

"Great, Kenneth. This kind of stuff isn't always easy to admit. But, realizing there might be a problem is the first step to change. Now let's go over the rest of the questionnaire. And be assured, we'll take a look at Sally's."

Dr. Douglas concludes his review of Kenneth's questionnaire and moves on to Sally's questionnaire.

SALLY'S PARENTING SCHEMA QUESTIONNAIRE

__3__ **Anxious-Attachment:** I often worry about whether my child loves and likes me. I also worry about whether I could go on if anything happened to my child.	__0__ **Avoidant-Attachment:** I believe kids are to be seen and not heard. I am uncomfortable with hugging and kissing. I don't feel my child needs to hear "I love you." I don't spend a lot of time with my kid.
__3__ **Blameworthy:** I never feel like I do a good job of parenting. If something goes wrong, I feel like it's all my fault. When my kid gets in trouble, I feel like it's all my fault.	__0__ **Blameless:** I hate admitting I made a mistake. When someone blames me for something, I usually find someone or something else to blame. When my kid gets into trouble, it's usually someone else's fault, certainly not mine.
__2__ **Naive:** I never worry about my kid getting hurt or getting into trouble. Everything always works out for the best. There's no reason not to trust people. I trust my child completely.	__0__ **Distrust:** I am a worry-wart. The world is a dangerous place. People are out to get you. I can't easily trust my kid. Even if I could trust my own kid, other kids are likely to get him or her into trouble.
__2__ **Other-Centered:** I can't do enough for my kid. My kid's needs are far more important than my own.	__2__ **Self-Centered:** My needs come first. Raising my child often feels like an intrusion in my life.
__0__ **Perfectionist:** I think if something is worth doing, it is worth doing perfectly. There is a right way and a wrong way to do things. I expect my child to hold to the same high standards I have for myself.	__3__ **Unambitious:** I don't worry at all about how well my kid does at school or anything else. As long as my kid gets by, that's good enough for me. It's stupid to put more effort into something than you have to.

__0__ **No Play:** Life is serious. Play is a frivolous waste of time. My child's worth will come from work.	__2__ **All Play:** The focus for my family is on having a good time. We play as much as we can. We only work to get the absolute essentials done. Life is meant for fun.
__0__ **Excessive-Control:** Nothing is more important than having strict discipline. Otherwise, a family would be utter chaos. My kid toes the line or else.	__2__ **No Control:** I can't say no to my kid. When I do make rules, I have a very hard time enforcing them, especially when my kid gets upset.

"Sally, I notice you gave yourself a three on Anxious-Attachment. You worry a lot about how your kids, and probably Kenneth, feel about you. Does that cause any problems in your family?"

"I guess I do try to make sure everyone is happy and that they like me. I'm afraid of making anyone mad at me. I realize I don't stand up for myself. Sometimes I would really like to get through to Kenneth, but I'm afraid he'll get mad. And sometimes I let the kids walk all over me when Kenneth's not around. The kids don't see me as a strong parent. Maybe that's another reason Lindsey felt she had no choice. She knew I wouldn't even try to get her dad to reconsider. Maybe she was even making a statement that she didn't want to be a wimp like her mother."

Kenneth turns to Sally. "You know, if you had talked to me, I probably would've had a hard time listening. Still, it would have been worth trying."

Dr. Douglas intercedes, "What the two of you did or didn't do in the past doesn't really matter. What's important is what we can do now to change things. Awareness of what's been going on is a great first step. At the next session, we'll finish going over your schema questionnaire, Sally, and then we'll roll up our sleeves and decide what we want to do about all of this."

Looking confused, Kenneth asks, "Okay, I can see some value in where we are headed, but doesn't Lindsey enter in here somehow?"

"Oh, I haven't forgotten about her, Kenneth. I definitely want to spend some time with her as well. I just find it useful to address the parent part of the equation first. Lindsey will also need to address some of her issues herself. After all, she's fifteen years old and bears some of the responsibility for how things are headed in her life, too."

You may already be able to see how schemas affect parenting. For example, Kenneth's harsh discipline stems from his Excessive-Control schema. Perhaps you can see where, in Kenneth's case, his Distrust schema also leads him to be extraordinarily strict. The fear of his children getting hurt or led astray by bad influences makes him overprotect. For Sally, Anxious-Attachment causes her to fear confrontation. She doesn't want to risk incurring rejection or disapproval from either Kenneth or her kids.

At this point, you may not understand all of the ramifications of your own parenting schemas. But seeing other people's parenting schemas in action can help you understand your own. Let's investigate some more of Jennifer's parenting schemas.

Jerod slams the alarm, groaning in the early morning light. Grabbing a towel from the floor, he stumbles into the shower. "Damn, another day of school," he mutters to himself. Drying off, he pulls on baggy pants and a baseball jersey. He makes his way gingerly through the maze of Leggos and toys strewn about the living room. "Damn, damn, damn," he swears, stubbing his toe on a plastic dollhouse.

Living with his father and his father's new family has not been a picnic for Jerod. His stepmom resents him and the kids are monsters. It doesn't feel like his home. He has to sleep on the sofa in the living room and has no privacy. A mess of toys litter the room, and the TV is usually turned to some stupid preschool show. As much as he hates to get up for school, morning is usually the only time Jerod has some peace in this house. His probation requires him to attend school every day and remain in his father's home the rest of the time. It's driving him crazy. He still can't get over the fact that his mom kicked him out.

Jerod drinks his orange juice and flips through a magazine. He gradually becomes aware of soft voices chanting something. "Oh great! The twins must be up," he thinks.

The chanting gets louder and he begins to make out the words. "Jerod is a jailbird. Jerod is a jailbird. Jerod is a jailbird." Louder. "Jerod is a jailbird. Jerod is a jailbird."

Leaping up, Jerod shouts, "Shut up, you little twerps! I'll kill you!"

"Jerod is a jailbird. Jerod is a jailbird," giggle four-year-olds

Sara and Alli. " Jerod is a jailbird. Jerod is a jailbird. Can't find us. Can't find us."

"I said, shut up!"

"Jerod is a jailbird. Jerod is a jailbird."

Jerod pulls the tablecloth up to find the girls squealing with delight under a table. "Jerod is a jailbird. Jerod is a jailbird."

"Damn it, I mean it. Shut the fuck up!"

"Oh, I'm telling my dad on you. You said a bad word!" Sara exclaims.

"Go ahead, you creep, he can't do anything to me."

"Don't you call my sister a creep," Alli counters.

"Shut up. You're both creeps. And I'm sick of you both." Jerod kicks the closest toy at the girls, grabs his backpack, and heads for the door.

"Mommy, Jerod hit us," a unison wail rises from under the table.

"That's it, I'm not taking anymore of this shit. See you around, creeps."

The next day, Jennifer is called to the phone at work. "Mrs. Dearborn, this is Trevor Wolfe again, your son's probation officer. Look, I know you said you didn't want anything to do with Jerod. But, Mrs. Dearborn, he's in the D-home again. I think he had a really hard time at his father's house. It really wasn't all his fault. He didn't have his own bedroom, the house was set up for little kids, and his stepmom and father couldn't cope with an adolescent. So Jerod took off, ditched school, and was picked up at the mall. I can't tell you how awful it is for him in the D-home. Unfortunately, there are quite a few gang members into much more serious activities. We're talking about murder, rape, and assault, Mrs. Dearborn. Jerod is terrified of them. He doesn't belong in here, but there's nowhere for him to go unless you agree to take him back. By the way, I know of a new therapist in town who takes a very different approach to dealing with these kinds of problems."

Jennifer has missed her son terribly. She's relieved to consider a different approach. She musters the strength to give it one more try.

When she goes to see her new therapist, Pam Warren, clinical social worker, Pam asks Jennifer to fill out a Parenting Schema Questionnaire. The next week, Pam greets Jennifer, "Great, you filled it out. Let's see what you've got."

JENNIFER'S PARENTING SCHEMA QUESTIONNAIRE

__4__ **Anxious-Attachment:** I often worry about whether my child loves and likes me. I also worry about whether I could go on if anything happened to my child.	__2__ **Avoidant-Attachment:** I believe kids are to be seen and not heard. I am uncomfortable with hugging and kissing. I don't feel my child needs to hear "I love you." I don't spend a lot of time with my kid.
__3__ **Blameworthy:** I never feel like I do a good job of parenting. If something goes wrong, I feel like it's all my fault. When my kid gets in trouble, I feel like it's all my fault.	__0__ **Blameless:** I hate admitting I made a mistake. When someone blames me for something, I usually find someone or something else to blame. When my kid gets into trouble, it's usually someone else's fault, certainly not mine.
__0__ **Naive:** I never worry about my kid getting hurt or getting into trouble. Everything always works out for the best. There's no reason not to trust people. I trust my child completely.	__2__ **Distrust:** I am a worrywart. The world is a dangerous place. People are out to get you. I can't easily trust my kid. Even if I could trust my own kid, other kids are likely to get him or her into trouble.
__3__ **Other-Centered:** I can't do enough for my kid. My kid's needs are far more important than my own.	__2__ **Self-Centered:** My needs come first. Raising my child often feels like an intrusion in my life.
__3__ **Perfectionist:** I think if something is worth doing, it is worth doing perfectly. There is a right way and a wrong way to do things. I expect my child to hold to the same high standards I have for myself.	__0__ **Unambitious:** I don't worry at all about how well my kid does at school or anything else. As long as my kid gets by, that's good enough for me. It's stupid to put more effort into something than you have to.

__0_ **No Play:** Life is serious. Play is a frivolous waste of time. My child's worth will come from work.	__0_ **All Play:** The focus for my family is on having a good time. We play as much as we can. We only work to get the absolute essentials done. Life is meant for fun.
__0_ **Excessive-Control:** Nothing is more important than having strict discipline. Otherwise, a family would be utter chaos. My kid toes the line or else.	__4_ **No Control:** I can't say no to my kid. When I do make rules, I have a very hard time enforcing them, especially when my kid gets upset.

They review Jennifer's Parenting Schema Questionnaire in detail. Jennifer, for the first time, begins to understand the issues that have hampered her parenting and provided fertile ground for Jerod's misbehavior. After going over the list, together they decide to target her Perfectionist schema first. They plan to explore the origins of her perfectionism and later decide on the next steps. Pam cautions Jennifer not to expect great changes right away. Jennifer leaves the session, feeling hopeful for the first time in years.

Jennifer is an example of a parent who very much wants to make changes in herself if it will help her child. And Kenneth, though not a believer in therapy, would do anything for his kids. Unfortunately, not every parent is equally motivated. And some acknowledge their shortcomings, but think it's impossible to change. They say you can't teach an old dog new tricks. That belief represents a way of avoiding the anxiety involved with change. Declaring change as impossible allows you to avoid both the fear of change and the responsibility for making it. And some parents avoid responsibility by blaming others.

For years Debra blamed the school for Quinton's problems. When Dr. Chavez, the school psychologist, invited her to spend a few sessions discussing Quinton's problems, she agreed. She felt sincere at the time, but her defensive style was firmly back in place by the time of her first appointment.

Debra arrives at her appointment thirty-five minutes late. Dr. Chavez, looking down at his watch, remarks, "Debra, we only have fifteen minutes left in our session. But we can accomplish something."

"What do you mean? I thought we'd spend an hour together. My cleaning lady was late. I had to wait for her."

Dr. Chavez explains, "Everyone has things that get in the way sometimes. I certainly understand. However, I have scheduled appointments. Let's get started. Do you have the questionnaire from last week?"

"I filled out the questionnaire you gave me at the school meeting, Dr. Chavez. Frankly, I found it a little silly. I just don't see where any of this has to do with me or my son. I'm not mentally ill."

Dr. Chavez responds, "It may not make much sense to you right now, Debra, but let's take a look at what you came up with."

DEBRA'S PARENTING SCHEMA QUESTIONNAIRE	
__1__ **Anxious-Attachment:** I often worry about whether my child loves and likes me. I also worry about whether I could go on if anything happened to my child.	__2__ **Avoidant-Attachment:** I believe kids are to be seen and not heard. I am uncomfortable with hugging and kissing. I don't feel my child needs to hear "I love you." I don't spend a lot of time with my kid.
__2__ **Blameworthy:** I never feel like I do a good job of parenting. If something goes wrong, I feel like it's all my fault. When my kid gets in trouble, I feel like it's all my fault.	__2__ **Blameless:** I hate admitting I made a mistake. When someone blames me for something, I usually find someone or something else to blame. When my kid gets into trouble, it's usually someone else's fault, certainly not mine.
__1__ **Naive:** I never worry about my kid getting hurt or getting into trouble. Everything always works out for the best. There's no reason not to trust people. I trust my child completely.	__1__ **Distrust:** I am a worrywart. The world is a dangerous place. People are out to get you. I can't easily trust my kid. Even if I could trust my own kid, other kids are likely to get him or her into trouble.

__2_ **Other-Centered:** I can't do enough for my kid. My kid's needs are far more important than my own.	__2_ **Self-Centered:** My needs come first. Raising my child often feels like an intrusion in my life.
__0_ **Perfectionist:** I think if something is worth doing, it is worth doing perfectly. There is a right way and a wrong way to do things. I expect my child to hold to the same high standards I have for myself.	__0_ **Unambitious:** I don't worry at all about how well my kid does at school or anything else. As long as my kid gets by, that's good enough for me. It's stupid to put more effort into something than you have to.
__0_ **No Play:** Life is serious. Play is a frivolous waste of time. My child's worth will come from work.	__2_ **All Play:** The focus for my family is on having a good time. We play as much as we can. We only work to get the absolute essentials done. Life is meant for fun.
__0_ **Excessive-Control:** Nothing is more important than having strict discipline. Otherwise, a family would be utter chaos. My kid toes the line or else.	__2_ **No Control:** I can't say no to my kid. When I do make rules, I have a very hard time enforcing them, especially when my kid gets upset.

"Well, Debra, it does look like you feel none of these issues pertain to you in any major way. Sounds like, in general, you feel as if your parenting isn't too affected by these issues. But you did give yourself a few two's. I usually find it useful to take a look at those and to see if they actually do need attention. And sometimes, the numbers need to be adjusted once we've looked them over more carefully. Why don't we go over a few of these?"

"I still think Quinton's teachers have more problems than I do, but if you think it's important, I've set aside this hour already."

"Great, Debra. Let's start with the No Control schema. You say you find it hard sometimes to say no to Quinton. Can you give me an example of that?"

"Well, sometimes he wants to stay up late and I let him. But I really don't think that's a very big deal."

"Tell me about one specific time that happened."

"I remember last week, he wanted to watch TV and I said no. But then he started to beg."

"So, what did you do next?"

"Well, I raised my voice and said no, but he kept at it. Frankly, I just got sick of his noise and figured it wasn't that big of a deal."

"So, Debra, what do you think the message to Quinton might have been?"

"Well, it's no big deal. I just let him stay up an hour. What are you getting at?"

"I'm concerned that Quinton may be learning that if he keeps on whining and complaining, that he'll get his own way."

Debra laughs. "Well, that's true isn't it? Doesn't the squeaky wheel get the oil? It works for me all the time."

Dr. Chavez can't contain a smile. "Sometimes it's appropriate to be the squeaky wheel, but Quinton seems to be doing it at school too much."

"I disagree. In this day and age, people have to be assertive to get what they want. Otherwise, people walk all over you."

Feeling frustrated, Dr. Chavez attempts to refocus the discussion, "Let's go back to the issue of limit setting and problems exerting control. Can you think of any other times that you've given in to Quinton?"

"I guess sometimes I end up finishing his homework. He puts it off until the last minute and doesn't have the time to finish. It isn't worth the hassle of pleading with him to do it. And I don't want to keep him up past his bedtime."

"Gosh, Debra, can you see where that could be a problem?"

"No. The teachers don't realize how smart Quinton is; they load him up with stupid busy work. It's a waste of time and it bores him."

"How about one more example of when you've given in to Quinton?"

"I try to make him eat healthier food. But he really doesn't like it and when I try to feed him healthy food, he throws a fit. So, I figure it's better for him to eat something than nothing. I end up buying a lot of chips, sodas, and candy so he won't starve to death."

"And I would guess that you don't see this as much of a problem either, am I right?"

"I'm sure he'll grow out of it."

"Debra, let's not worry yet about whether this saying no thing is a big problem or not. What I'd like you to do is simply write down each time you start to say no but ultimately give in. Maybe we'll decide it's not a huge problem. Or maybe it will end up looking a little worse than it does to you right now. Try to be patient with me on this. Frankly, I think that looking at this stuff is a lot harder than you realize. And I want you to know your parenting isn't on trial here. We both want the best for Quinton. Does the task of writing down these episodes sound okay to you?"

"Sure, as I said before, I want what's best for Quinton."

Debra represents a challenge for Dr. Chavez. Although she doesn't admit to any responsibility at this point, Dr. Chavez knows that has to do with her Blameless schema. Blameless people block out negative data. Dr. Chavez realizes he has to carefully gather evidence in a nonthreatening manner. He also suspects that Debra's lateness may be a way to avoid revealing painful aspects of herself, while reflecting a poor sense of limits and boundaries. In his work with her, he maintains a keen awareness of her various defenses. It will take time for her to develop an accurate list of her parenting schemas and then to see the effect they have on her son. And he knows progress will proceed slowly.

What Parenting Schemas Do to Your Kids

You've rated yourself on the Parenting Schema Questionnaire and seen how some of these schemas play out with our three families. It's equally important to know what effect schemas have on your children. It may surprise you to learn that the same schema can have opposite effects on kids. For example, a parent with Excessive-Control schema (like Kenneth) may end up with kids who are extremely compliant and fearful of misbehaving. On the other hand, the kids might do the opposite by rebelling, as Lindsey did. While this reactionary effect is common, opposite schemas sometimes have identical effects on kids. For example, a parent with a Perfectionist schema may keep a perfect house and have a child who mimics that behavior. However, a parent with an Unambitious schema who cares little about housekeeping may also end up with a child who acquires perfectionistic standards. This child may feel embarrassed by the sloppiness of the home and react with a need to "do better."

In the following table, we list each pair of parenting schemas and their frequent effects on kids. As you know, kids often try to imitate or model their parents or other important people in their lives.

And psychologists have come up with a predictable term for this kind of learning—modeling. Another way children learn is through what psychologists call reinforcement. In other words, children learn to do something more often when they are rewarded for doing it. These rewards can be praise and approval, special privileges, money, presents, and so on.

Many times children acquire the schemas of their parents. But not always. Sometimes they develop the opposite schema. Of course, we can't always predict the effect of every parenting schema. That's because other factors such as genetics, temperament, peers, teachers, and culture enter in. Nevertheless, these effects easily result when extreme parenting schemas exist.

THE EFFECTS OF PARENTING SCHEMAS ON CHILDREN			
Parental Schemas	**Potential Resulting Schema in Child**	or	**Potential Resulting Schema in Child**
Anxious-Attachment	Children may become anxiously attached because of their parents' constant anxiety.	or	Children may become avoidantly attached because of feelings of having been smothered.
Avoidant-Attachment	Children may become anxiously attached because of their parents' emotional unavailability.	or	Children may become avoidantly attached as a protection against the hurt of emotional unavailability.
Blameworthy	Children may engage in self-blame to protect their parents or because of modeling and/or reinforcement.	or	Children may become blameless because their parents take on all the blame.

Blameless	Children may engage in self-blame because their parents blame them so much.	or	Children may overly avoid blame because of modeling and/or reinforcement.
Naive	Children may become naively overly trusting because of modeling and/or reinforcement.	or	Children may become excessively distrusting because their parents do not provide adequate protection.
Distrust	Children may become overly trusting because their parents have excessively protected them.	or	Children may become overly distrusting due to modeling and/or reinforcement.
Other-Centered	Children may become other-centered due to modeling and/or reinforcement.	or	Children may become self-centered due to spoiling by their parents.
Self-Centered	Children may become other-centered because their parents expected the kids to please them.	or	Children may become self-centered due to modeling and/or reinforcement.
Perfectionist	Children often become perfectionists due to modeling and/or reinforcement.	or	Children become sloppy because their parents' perfectionism causes excessive pressure.

Parental Schemas	Potential Resulting Schema in Child	or	Potential Resulting Schema in Child
Unambitious	Children become perfectionists because they can't stand their own parents' sloppy approach to the world.	or	Children become sloppy due to modeling and/or reinforcement.
No Play	Children learn excessive seriousness due to modeling and/or reinforcement.	or	Children learn to play to excess in rebellion to the misery of their parents' seriousness.
All Play	Children learn excessive seriousness in response to their parents' frivolous, shallow lifestyle.	or	Children learn to value play well above work due to modeling and/or reinforcement.
Excessive-Control	Children may learn to become excessively compliant due to reinforcement and/or modeling.	or	Children may become rebellious in reaction to the excessive limits set by their parents.
No Control	Children may learn to become excessively compliant due to a yearning for limits.	or	Children may become out of control due to a lack of limits set at home by their parents.

While we can't capture the full complexity of the influence of parents' schemas on their children in the chart above, the essence is expressed. You can see that opposite schemas easily cause the same results in children, and that the same schema can cause opposite results.

In Summary

In this chapter you assessed your own parenting schemas. Though you've completed your Parenting Schema Questionnaire, remain open to reexamining them as you collect more data. This is because as your awareness increases, so will your accuracy in rating your behaviors and feelings. For example, in Debra's case, you have yet to see her ultimate parenting schema ratings because she has further work to do before she can complete that task accurately. If you find yourself struggling with your child, write down what the struggle was about and look over your Parenting Schema Questionnaire to see if one of those schemas might be playing a role.

Next, you learned about the effects parents' schemas often have on their children. Again, these effects are not inevitable because so many other things influence children. What we find fascinating is that, especially at the extremes, the same parenting style can cause opposite effects in children, and opposite parenting styles can cause the same exact results in children. The only way out of this puzzling impasse is to find the Middle Way.

More Practice

Identify three of your problematic parenting schemas. In the chart below, write the name of each schema along with its definition. Then think about how the schema may be affecting your child. If you need help, refer back to the table titled "The Effects of Parenting Schemas on Children" for ideas.

How Schemas Affect Your Children

Schema label: _____ Definition: _____	How I think this schema is affecting my child: _____ _____ _____ _____ _____ _____ _____
Schema label: _____ Definition: _____	How I think this schema is affecting my child: _____ _____ _____ _____ _____ _____ _____
Schema label: _____ Definition: _____	How I think this schema is affecting my child: _____ _____ _____ _____ _____ _____ _____

Chapter 4

Getting Rid of Guilt

Taking Responsibility for Change

Acceptance

Social worker Pam Warren asks Jennifer, "Have you had time to think about what we talked about last week? I recall our plan for this week was to explore the roots of some of your schemas. What thoughts have you had about that?"

"Oh, I haven't stopped thinking about our last session. I realize all of Jerod's problems are my fault. I gave in too easily to his demands and spoiled him rotten. I couldn't stand him failing anything so I did everything. I wanted the house to look perfect so I always cleaned his room. I never expected him to do anything. I see how that's ruined his life. I've been a horrible mother. No wonder the poor kid is in so much trouble. I haven't slept all week. I can't stand myself."

"Now, hold on, Jennifer. Let me tell you something about self-blame. Actually, I'm glad this came up right now because it fits in with what we need to talk about today. It's common when people begin to work on their core emotional issues for them to berate themselves. Sometimes, it borders on what I would call self-abuse. Self-abuse is a trap. What we really want to do is work on change. Self-abuse stops change dead in its tracks."

"How can I not blame myself? It *is* my fault. I raised Jerod. And I'm the one who screwed up. Just look at him. Nobody wants him. I doubt he's passing in school. He doesn't have any real friends. He's just miserable. He'll never be happy." Jennifer's shoulders slump as she looks down, puts her hand over her eyes, and softly sobs.

"I can tell you really love your son, Jennifer. Watching him go through this must be terribly painful." Pam offers Jennifer a tissue.

Collecting herself, Jennifer wipes her tears. "It is hard, Pam. I feel so guilty."

"Yes, he has problems, Jennifer. And you indeed contributed to them. I'm curious though: About what percentage of Jerod's problems do you feel responsible for?"

Jennifer crosses her legs tightly and shifts in her seat. "Wow. I guess it would be most of it. After all, I raised Jerod myself. Probably ninety percent. It really is mostly my fault."

"I understand you feel that way. I can see how much that thought hurts you. For the moment, let's switch gears. I want to do something different. Forget Jerod for the moment. Let's think about a hypothetical kid. Pretend he's about Jerod's age. We'll call him Joseph. Joseph's mother had quite a few problems. And her parenting wasn't exactly great. Joseph was a mess. Obviously, his mom's parenting caused some of his problems, but she wasn't entirely to blame. Let's list all of the other factors that might have gone into the pot that ultimately created Joseph. We'll call it our Recipe for Child Development."

"So what do you mean? Things like his father?"

"Oh, that's a very good one, Jennifer. His father must have influenced him a great deal. Even if the father wasn't around, that fact alone had to impact Joseph. Can you think of other ingredients that belong in the recipe?"

"Well, I guess his friends. And, of course, other relatives. Possibly school and church."

"Excellent. In fact, Jennifer, new research indicates that for many kids, friends influence them about as much as their parents. I was trained to think a good home life could overcome anything. Now it appears that isn't so. Let me throw in another ingredient to our recipe. Research on twins raised apart suggests genetics and biology account for about fifty percent of an individual's personality. Temperament is one part of our personalities that's genetic. Everyone comes into the world with a predisposition for a certain type of temperament. Some of us are shy, others outgoing. Some are easygoing and others are quite tense and anxious. Some deal with change easily while others struggle with change."

"Jerod was like that. He couldn't handle any disruption in his routine from the day he was born."

"That's what I'm talking about. Jerod was born with that trait. It was nothing anybody did to him; genes caused it. And that kind of temperament presents special challenges. But let's not get distracted. Temperament isn't the only biological factor. Genes also influence intelligence, health, and appearance. Appearance is important because research has demonstrated that good-looking children get treated better by peers and teachers than less attractive children. Another ingredient in our child development recipe might be culture."

"Right, culture and all the stuff kids see on TV and movies. I can't believe how much violence they're exposed to."

"That's true, Jennifer. Research strongly suggests that TV violence isn't doing our kids much good. Also, the pressures on modern families, such as divorce, frequent moves, and variable child care quality in the early years all spice up our recipe. So let's review our list."

RECIPE FOR CHILD DEVELOPMENT

Relationships	Biology	Social	Modern Pressures
mother father other relatives friends	temperament intelligence appearance health	culture school church	TV movies newspaper divorce child care quality family moves

Jennifer sighs. "I guess I know where you're headed with this, Pam. You want me to realize that I'm not exactly one-hundred percent responsible for Jerod's problems."

Pam laughs. "Well, then, I don't have to give you the long version of my spiel. You get the point, don't you? And we forgot one very important ingredient. Don't children eventually have to assume some of the responsibility for how they live their lives?"

"Sure they do, but I feel bad about my part of it."

"Of course you do. But, tell me, now that we've gone over our Recipe for Child Development, what percentage of Jerod's problems resulted from your parenting as opposed to everything else?"

"Well, obviously, I couldn't possibly have caused more than twenty or twenty-five percent of it. Genetics, his friends, and lots of other things made Jerod who he is. Still, I feel really bad about the part I added to it."

"I know you do. That's because you're a caring parent. But I think it's important for you to understand that you did the best you knew how to do. You came by your parenting problems honestly. As we discussed before, your schemas got in the way of your parenting. We both know your perfectionism had a negative impact on Jerod. It caused you to not let Jerod make his own mistakes and deal with them himself. If he screwed up his homework, you did it for him. If he didn't make his bed right, you redid it. But, you didn't ask for your schemas. Just as you take some responsibility for Jerod's problems, your parents and the other ingredients in our Child Development Recipe created you. Let's take a look at the roots of your perfectionism."

"So it never ends. Jerod blames me, I blame my parents, and they blame their parents. What's the point?"

"The point is, when you understand the origins of your issues, you can stop blaming yourself. Or anyone else for that matter. It isn't about blame. It's about self-acceptance. When you fully understand where your problems stem from, you can stop beating yourself up. When you engage in self-abuse, there's no energy left for making changes. And change requires vigorous effort."

Pam and Jennifer went on to probe the developmental roots of Jennifer's Perfectionist schema. Through that process, Jennifer began to see that her intense desire for attention and love from her parents caused her to strive for perfection. In reviewing her past, she relived some of the disappointment and pain of her childhood. But that pain helped her gain a deeper appreciation for how she had become who she is today. As her understanding grew, so did her fledgling self-acceptance.

Pam was trying to do two things. First, she helped Jennifer see that she was not solely responsible for Jerod's problems. Obviously Jerod's father and their divorce created difficulties. Also, Jerod's friends, his school, and his culture exerted influence. So did his temperament, genetic makeup, and various other experiences. Second, Pam wanted Jennifer to know that what responsibility she did bear had understandable causes. Jennifer's own problems stemmed from her early experiences and the same kind of influences Jerod had. Both of these strategies were designed to foster self-acceptance.

Self-acceptance is impossible when you're mired in self-blame and/or self-abuse. We aren't suggesting you should not assume responsibility for your parenting problems. Responsibility and blame have little in common. Blame only depletes your emotional reserves. It causes self-pity and depression. Depressed, self-loathing people don't do anything. By contrast, responsibility points the way toward action, because it doesn't burden you with negative emotion. Responsibility allows you to own your part (but *only* your part) of the problem and invites realistic self-acceptance. It's very hard to make changes until you achieve self-acceptance. Self-acceptance is a crucial part of the change process; trying to skip it is like trying to drive your car on an empty tank of gas. You won't go very far.

Responsibility

Debra, on the other hand, has no problem with self-blame. Quite unlike Jennifer, Debra blames everyone else for Quinton's problems. Debra accepts herself but fails to accept responsibility. Without accepting responsibility, she has no reason to change. *In order to change your parenting, you must accept yourself and also accept responsibility.* Sometimes it's a tricky balance to strike. Dr. Chavez has his work cut out for him in dealing with Debra.

"I'm here to see Dr. Chavez," Debra announces to the school secretary.

"Okay, please have a seat. You're about thirty minutes early."

"Well, I don't have time to sit around here for half an hour. Can't you let him know I'm here?"

"He's in with a student. I'll let him know when he gets out."

"What do you expect me to do for thirty minutes? Students are here all day. Can't he see the student later?"

Surprised, the secretary looks at Debra quizzically. "Ah, you're asking me to interrupt? I can't do that."

Both turn around as Dr. Chavez and his student come out of his office. "Thank God, you're finally free," Debra exclaims.

"Actually, Debra, I need to walk this young man back to class and consult with a couple of teachers. Our appointment is for ten o'clock. I'll be back by then."

"All right, I guess I'll go and get a cup of coffee."

Dr. Chavez is not surprised at ten when Debra does not appear. Ten minutes later, she arrives. "Sorry, I'm late again. I saw one of my friends at the coffee shop across the street."

"Debra, I've noticed that showing up at the right time seems to give you trouble."

"I guess I just don't have the hang-ups about time that a lot of people do."

"Actually, Debra, it makes me wonder if you don't pay enough attention to how your lack of concern for time might affect others."

"I guess I'll have to think about that. Although some people get way too uptight about such things."

Choosing not to spend too much of the session on this issue, Dr. Chavez moves on.

"I see from my notes on last week's session that you were going to write down each time you had difficulty saying no to Quinton. How did that go?"

"Well, it never happened, Dr. Chavez. Quinton and I had a good week. There were no problems."

"I'm glad you had a good week. As you know, I receive Quinton's weekly progress reports from his teacher. I noticed his last report indicated several missing assignments. And under 'Parent Contact' it's noted that the teacher called you about this problem and that you told her you would take care of it. Did you manage to do that?"

"I had a lot to do this week. For heaven's sakes, Dr. Chavez, this is fifth grade we're talking about, not Harvard Law School. The kid won't die if he misses a few assignments. Why is this such a big deal?"

"I'm afraid Quinton basically told his teacher the same thing, Debra. He told her that his mom said, 'This is fifth grade, not Harvard Law School.'"

Debra laughs. "What a kid! He's got a great sense of humor, and he's not about to let anybody push him around."

Dr. Chavez looks alarmed. "Debra, if this attitude continues, he'll never be accepted at Harvard Law School or, for that matter, the county community college. People in the adult world don't get to pick and choose which assignments they complete. The foundation for lifelong work ethics gets constructed now."

"I'm not sure I agree with you, Dr. Chavez. People work far too much nowadays. And that homework is just busy work."

Debra and Dr. Chavez turn toward the door, hearing soft knocking. The door opens slightly. "Excuse me, I'm sorry, Dr. Chavez. I know you don't like to be interrupted during a session, but Quinton has just been sent to the principal's office and he's making quite a commotion. I thought you'd want to know."

"Thanks, we'll check on him in a minute."

Debra rolls her eyes. "I'm so tired of the way they jump on Quinton here. See, they're out to get him. He's a good kid. A little rambunctious maybe, but boys will be boys after all."

"Well, Debra, let's see what this is all about. I think . . ." Dr. Chavez stops as Principal Hansen storms through the door, Quinton in tow.

"I'm so glad you're both here. We have a major problem. This time he's gone too far. I'm afraid we're going to have to . . ."

Quinton brazenly breaks in, "She deserved it. Mom, you told me not to let anybody push me around! It was my turn. And she shouldn't have held on to the beaker like she did."

Debra stands. "What did they do to you this time, honey?"

Quinton jerks his arm free from the principal's grasp, "Leave me alone. Mom, it's not my fault! Can't you see how they pick on me?"

Pat Hansen's voice rises in exasperation, "Good grief, Debra! Quinton is really getting out of control. In science lab, he grabbed a glass beaker and threw it at a girl. It shattered against the wall and she's now in the emergency room with glass in her eye. The teacher said it was totally unprovoked."

Quinton interrupts, now shrieking, "The teacher always picks her first. It's not fair! I'm not going to let them push me around like this! You people don't like me."

Dr. Chavez stands. "All right, everybody settle down. One at a time. Quinton, you need to sit down and listen. No more interrupting. Everyone will get their turn to talk when I say so. Pat, do you know how the girl is doing?"

"We haven't heard yet, but our nurse was worried that the glass might have scratched her cornea."

Dr. Chavez shakes his head. "That could be serious. It could result in permanent eye damage. Debra, did you hear what Quinton just said? He said that he wasn't going to let people push him around. And do you see how he's always blaming the teachers? Where do you think he heard that message?"

"You mean from me?" she asks, defensively.

"Yes, Debra, can you tell the words are yours? I think Quinton is only repeating what he's heard."

Now visibly shaken, Debra says, "My God, I've created a monster. Maybe you're right. I need to be much harder on Quinton." Turning to Quinton, Debra screams, "Quinton! You are in big trouble! When we get home, you're going to be grounded for two months. No TV, no phone, no radio, no nothing. For the next two months, all you'll do is homework." She looks at Dr. Chavez. "Is that better?"

"Debra, I'm glad you can see you've been going in the wrong direction. That's good. But what we have to do is more complicated than leaping to the opposite extreme. We'll work out a whole game plan. And I certainly don't mean to defend Quinton. But it's important for us all to realize that he's learned this behavior and part of it stems directly from your parenting. It's going to take some time to teach both of you some new ways of being. I'm going to teach you all about the Middle Way of Parenting."

Dr. Chavez, unlike Jennifer's therapist, does not attempt to exonerate Debra. Rather than help her feel less guilty, he keeps her feet over the coals. Debra needs to assume some of the responsibility for Quinton's misbehavior. She's spent years warding off criticism of herself and Quinton. Dr. Chavez knows her dominant schema is Blameless. He doesn't particularly want Debra to feel consumed with guilt, but he knows she has to experience guilt and self-blame if she is going to be able to ultimately accept responsibility. Dr. Chavez also knows that Debra's newfound awareness of her role in Quinton's problems may be short-lived. Additional work will be required before her awareness solidifies.

Self-Acceptance

After several more sessions, Debra assumed a reasonable degree of responsibility for Quinton's problems. Now, she needs to learn self-acceptance. Again, it's important not to blame yourself excessively for your children's problems. Parents want what's best for their kids. Schemas residing outside of their awareness cause most parenting mistakes. In order to lead Debra to self-acceptance, Dr. Chavez decided to take the now more-cooperative Debra on an exploratory trip through her childhood. He did this to help her become more conscious of how schemas, learned decades ago, continue to affect her parenting today. We join them at a later session.

Dr. Chavez is pleased to see Debra arrive only seven minutes late. "Debra, when Quinton threw the beaker at the girl a few weeks ago, things got pretty intense, didn't they?"

"Yes, but it did really open up my eyes. I need to do something different, but I can't figure out what it is. Can you tell me what I should do, Dr. Chavez? What about that game plan you talked about?"

"I'm glad you're willing to work on your parenting. But first, let me ask you a question. Is it possible that even well before Quinton's incident, at least a part of you knew that you weren't doing the right thing? Did you know there were some things you should be doing differently, but found yourself driven to act the way you did?"

"Honestly, sometimes I did know I was defending Quinton and myself too much, but I couldn't stand to hear the criticism. I defended him before I even knew what I was saying. The words spewed out of my mouth. I don't know why. They just did. Sometimes I knew Quinton had done something wrong; I just couldn't admit it to other people."

"You've made a great leap forward here, Debra. Realizing you have a problem is the first step in the process of change. Now that you've started that process, it's time for us to look at where all this started. I'd like us to do something I call the Lifeline exercise. Over the past couple of decades of working with parents, I've found that how people parent almost always connects to how they were parented, along with other important childhood experiences. What we do with this exercise is write down significant memories from your childhood. Those memories usually give us clues concerning your parenting schemas and where they came from. Let's start with the earliest memory you have and go through about age sixteen. Does that sound okay?"

"Sure. You know, Dr. Chavez, last week I probably wouldn't have agreed to this. But now, I'm starting to think you know what you're doing."

He laughs. "Great. Let's begin. Tell me the first thing you remember and how old you were at the time. I'll write these down as we go."

"Well, I guess the first thing I can remember is when I was about four years old, I think. I remember holding on to the rail of my parents' boat. It seems like we were going too fast. The boat was bumping hard over waves and water kept soaking me. I'm pretty sure I was sunburned; my skin felt on fire and that made the water seem even colder. We must have been on Lake Erie. I was scared and crying. I think my sister was, too. I told my Dad to slow down again and again. I told him I was scared. But he just laughed. My mom was laughing, too."

"So you felt scared. Do any other thoughts and feelings come to mind?"

"I really felt alone. Like nobody was going to help me."

"Were there other times you felt like that?"

"Yeah. When I was little, my parents liked to party a lot. I remember lying in bed and hearing everyone laughing and talking until very late at night. Sometimes I'd sneak out and watch them.

I remember peering through the upstairs railing. No one ever noticed I was there. I felt lonely."

"Do you ever feel lonely now?"

"To be honest with you, I do feel empty. It's like I have everything I ever wanted. I have a beautiful house, a son, a husband who makes a great living and who gives me everything I want. And yet it doesn't make me happy. I try not to think about it too much." Dr. Chavez makes a mental note to explore this issue further at a later point.

"I want to talk about that sense of emptiness, Debra. But for the moment, let's continue the Lifeline. What else do you remember from childhood?"

"I remember when I was about seven years old, the fighting started. My dad would come home really late and he and Mom would yell at each other for a long time. Sometimes I'd come out of my room to see what was going on. My mom always looked mad and told me to go back to bed. Then my dad would say, 'It's all right, honey. Come sit on my lap.' He'd hold me really tight and tell me I was his favorite girl. His face was flushed and his breath smelled bad. I didn't like it. My mom usually stomped out of the room. I knew she was mad. And I felt funny. I don't know why."

"How did you feel about your dad? Were you close to him?"

"It seemed like my dad was always coming home from trips. He was a salesman. He was charming and good looking. He'd come barging into the house carrying lots of gifts. He seemed bigger than life, almost too big for the house. 'Girls,' he'd say, 'Daddy's home. Look what I brought you.' My sister and I would fly into his arms begging for our presents. He'd say, 'Hold on, my sweets, let me take a good look at you first.' We'd stand before him and he would spin us around always saying the same thing, 'I love my little girls.' We'd open our presents and give him a kiss. Funny, though, I hardly ever remember talking or doing anything with him. And the family boat rides had stopped long ago."

"Why do you think the boat rides stopped?"

"Mom always said it was because Dad was too busy with his customers. But I know why now."

"Why is that, Debra?"

"I'm pretty sure my dad fooled around a lot. He probably took other women on his boat. He was gone all the time. And my mom knew he wasn't always at work."

"Tell me about your relationship with your mother."

"She never had fun like my dad. By the time I was seven or so, she seemed depressed all the time. My mom was pretty when she was younger, but she gained so much weight over the years, you never would have known it. She didn't take care of herself. And she hardly ever did anything with us. It felt pretty lonely sometimes."

"I really hear the lonely theme. What else do you remember from your childhood?"

"You know, I was pretty unhappy myself. I've never really told anyone about it, but I was teased all of the time. It was awful," Debra said matter-of-factly.

"Tell me more about that. Who teased you and what was it about?" Dr. Chavez was concerned about Debra's nonchalant demeanor. She appeared almost as if in a trance, face drawn, eyes vacantly staring.

"Mom was not just a little overweight—she was the biggest woman most kids had ever seen. By the time I was in school, she'd stopped taking care of herself. Her hair was filthy and she wore these horrible Hawaiian dresses. Other kids teased me about her all the time. She didn't leave the house much, but when she did kids would point and laugh at me. They used to say, 'Here comes the mountain with her little hill.' At school my nickname was 'little hill.' It hurt really bad but I swore I'd never let them know that. I got really good at throwing back insults. I could get pretty vicious."

Debra's voice remained devoid of feeling. Dr. Chavez could only imagine the enormity of the pain Debra felt inside. "Wow, Debra, that must have been awful. Didn't any of your teachers come to your defense?"

"The teachers were no help. They didn't like me."

"Really? How come?"

"Well, I was so miserable, I wasn't much of a student. School work just didn't seem that important and, of course, I got no help at home. My mother was always eating in front of the TV and Dad was usually gone. The teachers started getting on me. They didn't try to help—they just got mad. Well, I can't believe I'm actually telling you this stuff. It's stupid really."

"It's not stupid at all, Debra. I think it's important. When the teachers got mad at you, how did you feel?"

"I was furious. Life seemed so unfair. I learned to get awfully good at making up excuses, and I learned to cheat."

"Cheat? How did you manage that?"

"I wasn't good in school, but I wasn't dumb. There were lots of ways to cheat and get out of work. I even learned to forge my mother's signature on notes so that I could ditch school. And when I was caught, I had a million lines; usually they worked."

"Debra, from what you've told me, you were a lonely child whose parents were not emotionally available. You were cruelly teased at school and no one came to your rescue. You were probably too upset to do your schoolwork. Since you weren't close to anybody, you learned to develop your own strategies for dealing with that. You learned to dodge responsibility, make up excuses, and keep to yourself. Who could blame you for that? You did the only thing you knew to do."

Debra suddenly begins to cry. "I never looked at it that way."

"I can see you're feeling really bad right now. Can you tell me more about what's going through your head?"

"I've never thought about how awful I felt as a kid. Talking about it brings it all back."

"Take a moment to think about it, Debra. I know it's painful, but how did you feel about yourself as a child?"

"I didn't feel very good about myself. Deep down, maybe I thought I was a bad person and I had to cover it up."

"There aren't very many really bad people, Debra. Most of us learn to be who we are from all of our experiences."

Dr. Chavez and Debra talk more about her difficult childhood. As they complete the task, Dr. Chavez continues, "Now let me show you what I want to do with all of this. Let's see what this history has to do with your parenting schemas. Remember that Parenting Schema Questionnaire I had you fill out? Let's take another look at it."

DEBRA'S PARENTING SCHEMA QUESTIONNAIRE

__1__ **Anxious-Attachment:**	__2__ **Avoidant-Attachment:**
I often worry about whether my child loves and likes me. I also worry about whether I could go on if anything happened to my child.	I believe kids are to be seen and not heard. I am uncomfortable with hugging and kissing. I don't feel my child needs to hear "I love you." I don't spend a lot of time with my kid.

__2__ **Blameworthy:** I never feel like I do a good job of parenting. If something goes wrong, I feel like it's all my fault. When my kid gets in trouble, I feel like it's all my fault.	__2__ **Blameless:** I hate admitting I made a mistake. When someone blames me for something, I usually find someone or something else to blame. When my kid gets into trouble, it's usually someone else's fault, certainly not mine.
__1__ **Naive:** I never worry about my kid getting hurt or getting into trouble. Everything always works out for the best. There's no reason not to trust people. I trust my child completely.	__1__ **Distrust:** I am a worrywart. The world is a dangerous place. People are out to get you. I can't easily trust my kid. Even if I could trust my own kid, other kids are likely to get him or her into trouble.
__2__ **Other-Centered:** I can't do enough for my kid. My kid's needs are far more important than my own.	__2__ **Self-Centered:** My needs come first. Raising my child often feels like an intrusion in my life.
__0__ **Perfectionist:** I think if something is worth doing, it is worth doing perfectly. There is a right way and a wrong way to do things. I expect my child to hold to the same high standards I have for myself.	__0__ **Unambitious:** I don't worry at all about how well my kid does at school or anything else. As long as my kid gets by, that's good enough for me. It's stupid to put more effort into something than you have to.
__0__ **No Play:** Life is serious. Play is a frivolous waste of time. My child's worth will come from work.	__2__ **All Play:** The focus for my family is on having a good time. We play as much as we can. We only work to get the absolute essentials done. Life is meant for fun.

__0__ **Excessive-Control:** Nothing is more important than having strict discipline. Otherwise, a family would be utter chaos. My kid toes the line or else.	__2__ **No Control:** I can't say no to my kid. When I do make rules, I have a very hard time enforcing them, especially when my kid gets upset.

"You said before that none of these issues had much to do with your parenting. But you did give yourself a two on Avoidant-Attachment, Blameworthy, Blameless, Other-Centered, Self-Centered, All Play, and No Control. From what we've discussed about your childhood, can you tell me what events might have contributed to some of these schemas?"

"Well, sure. I think my Avoidant-Attachment came from both of my parents. My dad never talked to me and my mother was too miserable to pay any attention. I guess I learned to keep my distance from people. You know, I really love Quinton, but maybe I haven't been very good at getting to know him."

"That's a really good insight, Debra. I know you love Quinton. Your parents didn't spend much time with you. So now maybe with Quinton it's hard for you to connect with him."

"I think it is. Maybe I should give myself a three on that one."

"How about the cruel teasing? And teachers didn't help you out. They were on your case, too. So, you learned to make up excuses for your behavior. When criticism came your way, you learned to throw it back at them. What schema do you think that might have fostered?"

"Ouch. You've got me on that one, Dr. Chavez. So you think I learned to become Blameless?"

"Well, what do you do whenever anyone criticizes you or Quinton?"

"This is hard. I'm really feeling anxious. My heart is pounding and my hands are sweaty." Debra nervously wipes her hands on her dress.

"You're right, Debra, this is very hard. Take a deep breath and let it out slowly." Debra breathes deeply and takes a moment to calm down. Dr. Chavez continues, "That's good. Often our bodies start to react when a particularly strong schema is challenged. I suspect this may be the case with the issue of feeling Blameless. What do you think?"

"I think I've turned Blameless into a lifestyle. It drives me nuts when people criticize either me or Quinton. Now, I can see where that comes from. You know, I suspect I should have given myself a four on Blameless. I really do hate admitting a mistake. And when Quinton gets in trouble, it's usually someone else's fault, certainly not mine." Debra sighs deeply and continues, "And maybe a three on Blameworthy, because down deep I think I've been trying to cover up all the bad parts of myself ever since childhood."

"You're doing good work, Debra. Now that you can see some of these things more clearly, how about we redo your entire Parenting Schema Questionnaire? And after that, we can take on changing your parenting for the better. You will be able to parent like you want."

Dr. Chavez has guided Debra through a process. First, he helped her to see she and Quinton were far from Blameless. Quinton's blatant misbehavior and modeling of Debra's own words helped penetrate the shield of blamelessness Debra usually held up. At that point she started to overreact with guilt, flipping into feeling Blameworthy. Then, Dr. Chavez carefully explored her childhood in order to help her more fully understand her parenting schemas. Initially, Debra continued to block her painful feelings from the past. But as it continued, Debra gradually became aware of her problematic patterns and where they came from, and she was able to break through the layers of denial that kept her from her painful emotions. Knowing the origins of her problems helped her to take a step toward accepting them and herself. Take a look at the revised Parenting Schema Questionnaire that Debra and Dr. Chavez completed.

DEBRA'S REVISED PARENTING SCHEMA QUESTIONNAIRE

__1__ Anxious-Attachment:	__3__ Avoidant-Attachment:
I often worry about whether my child loves and likes me. I also worry about whether I could go on if anything happened to my child.	I believe kids are to be seen and not heard. I am uncomfortable with hugging and kissing. I don't feel my child needs to hear "I love you." I don't spend a lot of time with my kid.

__3_ **Blameworthy:** I never feel like I do a good job of parenting. If something goes wrong, I feel like it's all my fault. When my kid gets in trouble, I feel like it's all my fault.	__4_ **Blameless:** I hate admitting I made a mistake. When someone blames me for something, I usually find someone or something else to blame. When my kid gets into trouble, it's usually someone else's fault, certainly not mine.
__1_ **Naive:** I never worry about my kid getting hurt or getting into trouble. Everything always works out for the best. There's no reason not to trust people. I trust my child completely.	__1_ **Distrust:** I am a worrywart. The world is a dangerous place. People are out to get you. I can't easily trust my kid. Even if I could trust my own kid, other kids are likely to get him or her into trouble.
__1_ **Other-Centered:** I can't do enough for my kid. My kid's needs are far more important than my own.	__3_ **Self-Centered:** My needs come first. Raising my child often feels like an intrusion in my life.
__0_ **Perfectionist:** I think if something is worth doing, it is worth doing perfectly. There is a right way and a wrong way to do things. I expect my child to hold to the same high standards I have for myself.	__0_ **Unambitious:** I don't worry at all about how well my kid does at school or anything else. As long as my kid gets by, that's good enough for me. It's stupid to put more effort into something than you have to.
__0_ **No Play:** Life is serious. Play is a frivolous waste of time. My child's worth will come from work.	__2_ **All Play:** The focus for my family is on having a good time. We play as much as we can. We only work to get the absolute essentials done. Life is meant for fun.

__0_ **Excessive-Control:** Nothing is more important than having strict discipline. Otherwise, a family would be utter chaos. My kid toes the line or else.	__4_ **No Control:** I can't say no to my kid. When I do make rules, I have a very hard time enforcing them, especially when my kid gets upset.

Visiting Your Childhood

Dr. Chavez also used an exercise commonly called a Lifeline. It's often useful to explore your childhood more completely. The following exercise will give you a way to do that.

Most modern approaches to psychotherapy don't spend countless months unearthing every nuance of one's childhood. Therapists typically focus on the here and now and solving problems of everyday living. At the same time, it's foolish to disregard the childhood origins of your current emotional issues. Learning about the origins accomplishes two things: First, you will more fully comprehend the schemas that get in the way of your parenting. And once you understand them, you'll more easily acquire self-acceptance.

One way to visit your childhood efficiently is to complete a Lifeline. A Lifeline consists of writing down emotionally significant (good or bad) memories from your past. Next to those memories, try to write a little about what thoughts and feelings you experienced at the time. If you don't remember what thoughts and feelings you had then, record the thoughts and feelings you have while reexperiencing those memories. Finally, go through your Parenting Schema Questionnaire from chapter 3 and try to match the experiences to your current problematic parenting schemas. Focus your efforts starting with your earliest memories to the age of about eighteen. Also include especially traumatic or emotionally powerful experiences after that.

LIFELINE EXERCISE			
Age	Memory	Thoughts and Feelings	Schema
First Memory			
Preschool Memories			
Grade School Memories			
Junior High/ Middle School Memories			

High School Memories			
Later Memories of Major Significance			

Once you have finished this exercise, go over your Parenting Schema Questionnaire again. You might find that some of the numbers need to be tweaked up or down. Debra reviewed her childhood and became more aware of her schemas. You also may find your own journey to the past clarifies why you often can't parent the way you want.

You've come to know Kenneth and read about some of his childhood experiences. We'll show you what a few of his memories, thoughts, feelings, and schemas look like on a Lifeline. Your own Lifeline should include more memories than this example, but Kenneth's partial sample can help you get a good sense of how to do your own Lifeline.

KENNETH'S LIFELINE			
Age	Memory	Thoughts and Feelings	Schema
six	My brother and I rode our bikes to a park, and someone stole mine while we were playing ball. My father had a fit. He told me I was lucky the person hadn't kidnapped and tortured us. He was always pointing out how dangerous the world can be.	I had nightmares about the man who stole my bike. For a while I was scared to leave the house.	Distrust
nine	I went hunting with Dad and my brother. My dad jumped all over me because I was so clumsy with a shotgun. He was really strict with me. He only gave me approval when I won at something or came out on top.	I thought I was inadequate. I felt ashamed and afraid. I learned to try to win at any cost. I didn't want my dad or brother to know how awful I felt so I learned to always act tough.	Excessive-Control
ten	On Christmas, my dad had promised me a train set. He gave me an encyclopedia. It seemed like he made promises all the time that he broke.	I learned never to trust what anyone promised. I felt betrayed and disappointed.	Distrust

| fourteen | I'd been given the job of cutting the grass. It was never good enough. I always missed a spot or didn't trim it well enough. I would look it all over until I was sure it was perfect. But my dad always came out and redid parts of it. | I felt angry and inadequate. Now, I'm glad my dad taught me that anything worth doing is worth doing right. | Perfectionist |

Obviously all of your memories won't fit neatly into a box that leads directly to one of your problematic schemas. You may find that some of your memories don't seem related to much of anything going on with you today. But if it is a powerful recollection, it probably connects to something important in your life. Look for patterns in your memories. Repeated, emotionally charged themes almost always create schemas.

In Summary

Why have we devoted so much space to acceptance and responsibility? Quite simply, it's because without striking some kind of balance between the two, it will be difficult for you to parent how you want. Remember, change is a demanding task. It will take great amounts of energy. Guilt consumes so much energy that you'll have little left for the task ahead. Take whatever time you need to find self-forgiveness and acceptance.

Parenting Practice

Reading about these issues will start you thinking about self-acceptance and responsibility. But actual learning requires action. Putting thoughts down on paper can clarify and focus your efforts.

Feel free to use the chart below for that purpose. In the first column, "Guilt," record one or more of the problems you have with parenting. In the second column, "Acceptance," use your Lifeline to help you figure out why you might have that problem, and try to think of something self-accepting to say. Finally, in the column "Responsibility," jot down your ideas for tackling that problem. Don't worry if your ideas aren't well-developed at this point. We'll give you lots more ideas later in the book. Look at the following example chart, and then you can do your own.

GUILT/ACCEPTANCE/RESPONSIBILITY		
Guilt (I feel bad about . . .)	**Acceptance** (I do this because . . .)	**Responsibility** (And here's what I'm going to do about it . . .)
I yell too much at my kids.	My mother yelled at me all the time. That was my role model. No wonder I do this.	1. Finish reading this book. 2. Take a stress management class. 3. Read about anger management.
I can't set limits with my kids. I cave in way too easily.	My parents were incredibly strict with me and I vowed never to do that to my kids. I went too far, but I had good intentions.	1. Finish reading this book. 2. Write down the things I want to set limits on to remind myself. 3. Ask my partner or friends for help when I feel weak.

GUILT/ACCEPTANCE/RESPONSIBILITY		
Guilt (I feel bad about . . .)	**Acceptance** (I do this because . . .)	**Responsibility** (And here's what I'm going to do about it . . .)

Chapter 5

BEYOND INSIGHT

Preparing for Action

Perhaps you're thinking, "Okay, okay, I understand my problematic parenting schemas and where they came from. I accept responsibility for them, and I can even accept myself for having them. So now what?" Unfortunately, many self-help books lead you to such insights and stop. And old-fashioned approaches to psychotherapy proceeded as though insight alone would solve any problem. That's about as foolish as learning that the reason you have trouble seeing is that you are nearsighted and having the thought, "Now that I understand what my problem is, it will get better on its own." Obviously, you need to take action and get glasses. Just *knowing* why you have poor vision won't do anything for you. And neither will knowing you have a few problematic schemas.

This chapter will help you take action. These early actions will help prepare you for making meaningful changes in your parenting. Some things might start to change at this stage, but don't expect a lot to happen immediately. Also, you will likely experience a few setbacks along the way. Lasting change takes time, patience, and persistence.

The Pace of Change

"So, how have things been going in your family this past week?" Dr. Douglas inquires.

Sally and Kenneth avoid eye contact by looking out the window. Finally Sally breaks the silence, "Not so good, Dr.

Douglas. Kenneth and I have been fighting all week. Lindsey won't talk to either of us."

Kenneth adds, "Well, at least Nick's doing fine. In fact, the school notified us that Nick is going to be considered for the gifted and talented program. It's nice to know we have one functioning member in this family. You know, I agreed to this therapy thing because Sally insisted. And that was fine. But we've been doing this three weeks now and things are just getting worse."

"Kenneth, do you invest in the stock market?"

Kenneth looks puzzled and irritated. "Obviously I have investments. So what? Are you trying to make sure you'll collect your bill?"

Dr. Douglas laughs. "Thanks for answering my question, Kenneth. Now answer this. Over time stocks generally go up. But have your investments gone up each and every week? Or for that matter every month?"

"Of course not. I invest for the long term. I know stocks grow over time, and it's stupid to worry about the daily ups and downs."

"So how about we invest for the long term in your family? Ups and downs happen the same way in therapy. If you hang in there, positive changes occur. They don't happen all at once and they never go straight up. Slips and slides in your progress are just as unpredictable in the short run as they are in the stock market. And the slips in therapy usually teach us valuable lessons, if we look at them carefully."

"Touché, Dr. Douglas. Have you ever thought about becoming an attorney?" Kenneth uncrosses his arms and settles more comfortably into his chair.

"Not really. I'm afraid I don't have the temperament for it." Dr. Douglas smiles. "Let's return to the topic you two first brought up. Tell me more about those fights you had last week. Sally, what do you think's going on?"

"It's pretty simple. We've been fighting over Kenneth's stupid Excessive-Control schema. He hasn't made any attempt to change his rules. He's just as strict as he always was. Poor Lindsey can't even breathe. He won't let her do anything. He admitted in our last session he wasn't getting the results he wanted, but he won't do anything about it."

Dr. Douglas turns to Kenneth. "No wonder you guys have been fighting this week. It sounds like our initial work has prompted Sally to start standing up to you and expressing her opinions. Apparently she's not letting her Anxious-Attachment schema stop her from speaking out. That must feel a little uncomfortable."

"Uncomfortable is an understatement. Sally's been all over me. And I'm not going to let Lindsey run wild. Maybe I haven't been doing the best thing, but I think if I let up on her, Lindsey's just going to get into more and more trouble."

"Remember, we discussed the fact you have an Excessive-Control schema, Kenneth. I'm not surprised you haven't taken steps to change it yet. At this point, you're firmly convinced that nothing is more important than having strict discipline. Without it, you're afraid your family would turn into utter chaos."

Kenneth nods in agreement.

Encouraged, Dr. Douglas continues, "Kenneth, you're a reasonable man. You're not going to change your approach without a good reason. I'd like to introduce you to a strategy you may be familiar with from your years of investing. It's called a cost/benefit analysis. Investors might call it a risk/reward ratio. Right now, you really fear if you stop controlling every detail of Lindsey's life, she'll get into serious trouble. That doesn't give you much incentive to change. But let's take a closer look at this issue. I'm going to divide this paper into two columns and title it, 'Kenneth's Excessive-Control Schema: Cost/Benefit Analysis.' Remember, your Excessive-Control schema means, 'Nothing is more important than having strict discipline. Otherwise, a family would be utter chaos. My kid toes the line or else.' Let's start with the benefits of this schema. How do you think it helps you?"

Kenneth ponders the question for a moment. "It should be obvious. I feel if I run a tight ship and maintain strict control, my family will be safer. Kids need guidance."

"Good start, Kenneth. What are some of the other benefits?"

"Kids nowadays run wild. If I don't control what they do, and when they do it, they'll fall prey to dangerous outside influences."

Sally interjects, "I thought we were here to *change* Kenneth's parenting. It sounds like we're encouraging him. What gives?"

"That's a legitimate concern, Sally." Dr. Douglas responds, "However, before anyone changes anything significant, they have to be convinced that the change is worthwhile. This exercise will help all of us see if changing this part of Kenneth's parenting makes sense. Now, Kenneth, can you think of any other benefits?"

"Through my discipline, the kids ultimately will learn self-discipline. Nothing has benefited me more than self-control. I never would have made it through law school without incredible sacrifice and willpower."

Dr. Douglas asks, "Anything else?"

"Yes. Respect. How else will kids learn to respect people in authority? My kids know I'm the boss. They respect me because of that. I think that just about covers it."

"Okay, Kenneth. Let's look at what I've written down."

KENNETH'S EXCESSIVE CONTROL SCHEMA: COST/BENEFIT ANALYSIS	
Benefits	**Costs**
1. I keep my children safe.	
2. I give my kids needed guidance.	
3. I keeps bad influences away from my kids.	
4. I teach them self-discipline and willpower.	
5. I teach my kids respect for authority.	

Kenneth looks over the cost/benefit analysis. "Okay. I suppose now you're going to tell me all the costs. But I don't see that there are any."

"No, Kenneth. I'm not going to tell you the costs. You're going to tell me what you see as costs. Sally, how do you feel about Kenneth's ultradisciplinarian approach?"

"You know I hate it. We have good kids. I can't stand the way he berates them. It makes me furious."

"So, Kenneth, would Sally's anger represent a cost?"

"If you want to call it that. I suppose so."

"I don't want to put it down as a cost unless you think it is. Does Sally's anger bother you?"

"Yes, of course. I don't like it at all. Yes, it's a cost."

"Okay, Kenneth. Now, how does Lindsey react to your limit setting?"

"Terribly. But that's the trouble with parents these days. They cave in. They simply want their kids to like them. That's not what parenting is all about."

Dr. Douglas nods. "I agree. Many parents don't discipline

when they should. However, right now, let's stick to the costs. How do you feel about Lindsey's anger toward you? Is that a cost? We'll worry about whether the cost is worth it later."

"Fine. I don't like Lindsey to feel that way. But I don't have that problem with Nick, he respects his father."

"So, Lindsey's anger might be a cost, but for Nick there is no apparent cost?"

"Yes, I'd agree with that."

"I'll jot that down then. Now, Kenneth, let's look at the incident that led you into therapy. Lindsey snuck out of the house, drank excessively, and ended up in an automobile accident with several adolescents who were drunk. What she did was wrong. And she's ultimately responsible for her behavior. Nevertheless, Lindsey reported that her actions stemmed in part from rebellion. She'd felt suffocated and resentful. Is it possible that one cost of exerting an Excessive-Control schema is rebellion?"

"Maybe in Lindsey's case. But not Nick. He's incredibly compliant. He does whatever I tell him. That's what I don't understand. I'm the same parent to both kids. So how can my parenting cause such opposite results?"

"That's a great question," Dr. Douglas responds. "The same parenting schema, at the extremes, often causes quite opposite results. Right now, Lindsey's acting out. But we mustn't forget Nick. Nick might have some problems of his own that we haven't had a chance to get into. I don't want to go too far astray from our cost/benefit task. But tell me, does Nick ever appear to be anxious or depressed?"

Sally, who had been listening but not participating, grips the arms of her chair and leans forward. "You know, I've been worried about Nick. Sure, he's a great student and he never misbehaves. But, lately, his appetite has gone down and he's been really irritable. Nick's always been a loner, but now I can't get him to do anything with his friends. He spends all his time in his room reading. I think he's afraid of Kenneth. He doesn't want to get into trouble like Lindsey."

"Nick's symptoms could be very serious. His overcompliance and fear may have led him into depression. I think it would be a good idea for me to see Nick by himself for a session. After we finish, be sure to talk to my secretary about making an appointment for him. Okay, back to costs. Kenneth, can you see where rebellion, as well as fear and overcompliance, could relate to overly strict parenting?"

"Look, first of all, there's nothing wrong with my son. You

shrinks are all alike. To you, everyone has a problem. I think you're way off with Nick. Maybe you have a point with Lindsey. I agree. She rebelled, okay?"

"All right, rebellion is a possible cost. And you don't see any problems with Nick, but Sally does. Looking at costs again, I remember at our last session you said that sometimes you feel pretty awful when you overreact and give consequences out of proportion to the crime. Does that feel like a cost?"

"I guess so. Yeah. Sure. Sometimes I feel pretty guilty. You know, I'm not sure I like what you're doing."

"Sometimes it does get a little uncomfortable Kenneth. Tell me if I'm pushing too hard."

"No, no. I'm tough enough to take it," Kenneth wryly retorts.

"I know you are Kenneth. Let's look at what your cost/benefit analysis looks like now."

KENNETH'S EXCESSIVE CONTROL SCHEMA: COST/BENEFIT ANALYSIS

Benefits	Costs
1. I keep my children safe.	1. Sally gets angry.
2. I give my kids needed guidance.	2. Lindsey gets angry.
3. I keeps bad influences away from my kids.	3. Lindsey became rebellious.
4. I teach them self-discipline and willpower.	4. Nick may be depressed.
5. I teach my kids respect for authority.	5. I feel guilty.

Kenneth, feeling a bit like he does in court when he's about to undercut the opposing attorney, argues, "Although I can see some costs, and they are indeed significant, I think you have to admit the benefits outweigh the costs here, Dr. Douglas. If you look at those costs, we're talking about some uncomfortable feelings. That's life. But now safety, self-control, respect, and guidance are crucial. No kid can live without them. You must agree with that."

"Yes, those are very important, Kenneth. I might not agree that feelings are insignificant, but for the moment, let's return to the benefit side of the equation. Your first benefit stated that your Excessive-Control schema helps keep your children safe. Did it manage to do that for Lindsey? And did it keep her away from bad influences?" Dr. Douglas inquires in a particularly gentle tone, realizing that Kenneth is now arguing a case in attorney mode.

"Jesus, you really should have been an attorney, Dr. Douglas. Point won. But, overall, I have kept them pretty safe. And I can't see stopping."

"That's true. You've shown wonderful concern for your kids' safety. I appreciate that. You know, you're a lot like many parents. When parents go to the extreme on one of their schemas, they usually act as though they have only one other option: the other extreme. For example, in your case, you seem to feel that you must either exert total control with severe limits or have no control at all. Yet is that really the only option? Is it possible for a child to grow up safely, with self-discipline and respect, in a family that exerts a little less control?"

"I suppose it could happen," Kenneth acknowledges.

"So you agree, it's possible. I wonder if moderate, though clearly enforced limits actually might provide those outcomes more reliably than severe limits. And without the costs. Moderate limits could defuse the resentment and anger your family experiences as well as the guilt you feel."

"I can see that might be possible. But without extreme limits, they're bound to make lots of mistakes. I can prevent that."

"You're right, they will make mistakes. And lots of them. Kenneth, have you ever made mistakes as an attorney? Sometimes even mistakes that you'd been warned about by your law professors? But that you committed anyway?"

"Of course, everyone does that early in their career."

"And after those mistakes, did you keep repeating them or did you learn something valuable. Perhaps something you couldn't have learned any other way? Did making the mistake and experiencing the consequences for it drive the lesson home? And isn't that true for kids also? No matter what their parents warn them about, kids often don't believe something until they've encountered the consequences of their own mistakes."

Sally interjects, "Kenneth, remember that trip to Arizona when the kids were little? We went on a hike through some Indian ruins. The ranger warned us about the dangerous thorns on some of the cacti. He told us that if we touched that particular plant, the thorn would embed itself so deeply we'd have to cut it out with a knife. Both of us warned the kids over and over. But Lindsey, you know how she is, couldn't resist. She tried to just barely touch it. We ended up going to the ranger's office for help. She sure never touched a cactus again."

Kenneth sighs. "I'm getting it from both sides now. All right, I concede. Maybe there is a better way. Maybe my Excessive-Control schema costs too much. What's next doctor?"

"If you really feel that way, what's next is for us to develop a plan for modifying this schema. We want to be careful not to throw the baby out with the bathwater. I don't want you to let your kids do anything they want. We'll need to collaborate on a middle-ground approach. For the next week, how about you simply write down all of the limits you enforce with the kids. We'll go over them together and make the changes we can all agree on. We're out of time for today. Don't forget to schedule an appointment for Nick."

Doing Your Own Cost/Benefit Analysis

Prior to conducting a cost/benefit analysis, Kenneth had little reason to change his parenting. Although his cost/benefit analysis helped him see some of the costs of his Excessive-Control schema, Kenneth needed coaching from Dr. Douglas to appreciate that the perceived benefits of this schema were largely an illusion. Only then could he see that the costs of his Excessive-Control schema outweighed the benefits. Now Kenneth is more ready and motivated for change.

You can do your own cost/benefit analysis. Choose a schema you rated as three or four on your Problematic Schema Questionnaire (chapter 3). First, list the benefits you associate with that schema. Try to be thorough. (If you're stuck, you may want to look at the examples provided in the following table.) You wouldn't have held on to your schema this long if you didn't believe there was some kind of benefit. Once you've listed your benefits, list the costs accrued by your schema. Be sure to include the effects on your relationship with your kids and/or partner. Finally, after you have listed all the costs and benefits you can think of, go through the list of benefits once more. Ask yourself whether those benefits could not be retained with a more moderate approach. And ask whether the benefits might be hollow. Almost anytime you subject the benefits of an extreme schema to scrutiny, the logic supporting them falls apart.

To help get you started, we have listed some of the costs and benefits parents frequently report for each of the problematic parenting schemas.

COMMON COSTS AND BENEFITS OF PARENTING SCHEMAS		
Schema	**Benefits**	**Costs**
Anxious-Attachment (afraid of losing others)	1. I give my kid lots of love. 2. I don't get into many fights. 3. If I'm vigilant, my kids might not leave me. 4. I protect my kids really well. 5. My partner never doubts my love.	1. Sometimes my kids feel smothered. 2. I don't always speak up for myself. 3. It makes me worry all the time about my kids. 4. It pulls me away from other relationships when I get too involved with the kids. 5. My partner feels smothered.
Blame-worthy (guilt is my middle name)	1. I'd rather take the blame for things than have my kids take the blame. 2. When I take the blame for things other people give me reassurance. 3. I don't have to work at my parenting because I know I'll never be able to do any better.	1. I feel guilty all the time. 2. My kids don't assume responsibility for their own actions, I do. That hurts them. 3. It keeps things stuck as they are; nothing ever gets better.

Schema	Benefits	Costs
Avoidant-Attachment (avoid intimacy and closeness)	1. I'm not dependent on love or attention from others. 2. I don't worry about what my kids are thinking. 3. I don't get hung up on getting affection from my kids.	1. I don't get to know who my kids are. 2. Sometimes I feel lonely or disconnected. 3. Other people say I'm missing out on something special from my kids.
Blameless (assume no responsibility, blame others)	1. I never have to feel guilty. 2. I don't have to change anything. 3. I can keep my kids out of trouble by blaming others for what they do. 4. I can blame my partner for everything that goes wrong.	1. Some people don't like me. 2. I get criticized for deflecting blame from my kids. 3. My kids aren't learning to assume responsibility. 4. My partner gets upset when I don't take responsibility when it's mine.
Naive (everything will work out)	1. I don't have to spend time worrying. 2. My kids know I trust them. 3. I don't have to plan ahead, everything always works out.	1. Sometimes my kids think I don't care about them. 2. I don't take enough precautions. 3. Since I don't plan ahead, I get surprised by occasional bad outcomes.

Schema	Benefits	Costs
Other-Centered (others' needs take center stage)	1. My kids get taken care of really well. 2. My kids will never grow up deprived like I did. 3. My kids get to feel special.	1. My kids seem spoiled to others. 2. I get exhausted taking care of them. 3. I never have time for myself. 4. Sometimes I feel resentful.
Perfection-istic (excessive standards)	1. I do things better than most people. 2. My kid can learn to value doing things right. 3. I am a role model for high standards.	1. My kids say I put too much pressure on them. 2. Sometimes I feel under a lot of pressure. 3. The family is always tense. 4. My kids say I'm too critical.
Distrust (the world is out to get me)	1. I can keep bad things from happening to my kids. 2. I plan ahead and avoid pitfalls. 3. I'm rarely disappointed because I anticipate the worst.	1. I worry all the time. 2. My kids complain that I don't trust them. 3. I miss opportunities because I don't take risks.

Schema	Benefits	Costs
Self-Centered (me, me, me)	1. I get my needs met.	1. My kids always complain that I don't do as much for them as other parents.
	2. I don't spend my whole life dwelling on taking care of my kids like other people do.	2. Sometimes I feel empty and I'm never completely satisfied.
	3. I have plenty of time for what I want.	3. My friends sometimes resent me.
	4. I demand my partner and children do anything and everything to make me happy.	4. My family sometimes gets tired of my demands.
Unambitious (lack of standards)	1. I don't get uptight like other people.	1. People criticize me a lot.
	2. I don't sweat the small stuff.	2. My kids feel embarrassed to bring anyone home.
	3. I don't have to work as hard as a lot of people.	3. My kids' teachers say I'm irresponsible.

Schema	Benefits	Costs
No Play (joyless, all work)	1. We get more important work done as a family.	1. My kids complain we never have fun.
	2. We don't waste time on frivolous things.	2. I'm not as happy as most people I know.
	3. My kids will learn how serious life is.	3. Sometimes I catch my kids laughing at something and as soon as they see me, they stop.
		4. My kids lie to get out of chores and sneak off with their friends.
All Play (party animal)	1. I have a lot of fun.	1. My kids don't do well in school.
	2. I know how to throw a good party.	2. I don't keep up with daily hassles like my checkbook very well, so sometimes checks bounce.
	3. My kids love to bring people home.	3. I inconvenience other people when I don't do my fair share.

Schema	Benefits	Costs
Excessive-Control (disciplin-arian)	1. My kids learn to toe the line.	1. My kids get resentful and angry with me.
	2. I keep my kids away from harm.	2. My kids sneak around.
	3. I keep my kids from making mistakes.	3. My kids rebel.
	4. I can teach my kids respect.	4. Sometimes I feel guilty when I overreact.
	5. My partner likes me to take care of the discipline.	5. My partner gets mad when I go overboard with discipline.
No Control (anything goes)	1. I don't have to tell my kids number	1. My kids are out of control and I don't know what to do.
	2. I don't fight with my kids.	2. My kids take advantage of me.
	3. My kid is my best friend.	3. People get really annoyed with my kids.
	4. My partner likes me to be easygoing.	4. My partner gets upset when the kids don't listen to me.

YOUR COST/BENEFIT ANALYSIS		
Schema	Benefits	Costs

After you have completed your cost/benefit analysis, feel free to do a few more on other problematic schemas. Just doing a cost/benefit analysis should make you more aware of the downsides to your problematic parenting schema(s). That act alone may initiate change, though more remains to be done. The following exercise will sharpen your ability to recognize your schema when it tries to corral your thoughts, feelings, and actions.

Self-Surveillance

Schemas thrive in dark places. Like roaches, they scatter when the light goes on. Simply turning on the light doesn't destroy them, but it temporarily gets them out of the way. Later, you can get an exterminator. This exercise turns on the light.

Putting a spotlight on schemas involves identifying all of their components. We'll briefly describe each component of the exercise and follow with Jennifer's Self-Surveillance exercise. Then you can start yours.

Sensations are the body's reactions to an emotional event. You will notice these first. They could include almost any physical response: tightness in your throat; upset stomach; rapid breathing or pulse; sweat; tears; flushed face; clenched fist; tightness in the shoulders, back, or neck; chills; nervous tapping; and so on. These reactions have a useful purpose. They tell you something is up, so you'll want to pay attention to them. Write them down as you notice them.

Feelings accompany sensations. Feelings are the words used to describe emotions. They include: sadness, fear, anger, joy, anxiety, embarrassment, pride, shame, guilt, disgust, love, hate, and exhilaration, among others. Sometimes feelings are hard to identify. For example, fear and anger often coexist even though you might only notice one of them. If you examine your bodily sensations, they can offer clues for identifying your feelings. For instance, if you find yourself crying in the middle of an argument, there may be elements of sadness or fear along with your anger. Be aware that you can have several feelings simultaneously.

Triggers are the events that precede sensations and feelings. Triggers come from other people, including your kids, partner, teachers, friends, or relatives. They can also come from television, the newspaper, or even your own daydreams. Anything that sets off a strong reaction in you is a trigger.

Thoughts are verbal statements you make to yourself about events in the world. They represent our interpretations and perceptions of triggers. They evaluate how important the trigger is and whether it is good or bad. *Thoughts are not always accurate.* Schemas distort thoughts. Thoughts are merely your perception of events. They are not facts. But it's important to track them.

Finally, schemas are the deeply held beliefs or lenses that you look at events through. They dictate your thoughts, feelings, and sensations. They also determine what events serve as triggers. Because they hide in the dark, you will need all of the other information above to illuminate them. This exercise might be the most difficult one in this book, and it's extremely important.

Jennifer started filling out Self-Surveillance charts after her third therapy session. Pam and Jennifer go over them together.

Pam hands Jennifer a glass of ice water. "How has your week been? Were you able to fill out the Self-Surveillance chart I gave you?"

"It's been a horrible week, Pam. I had more than enough triggers for my Self-Surveillance chart. I don't know if I did the right thing in taking Jerod back. He's been a disaster."

"I'm sorry to hear that, Jennifer. We've talked about the possibility that Jerod's behavior won't turn around. Only time will tell. The only thing we can control is how you react and how you think and feel. The Self-Surveillance chart will help us get that control. Let's look at what you wrote this last week."

"This wasn't easy to do. I'm not sure I filled it out right. But here's what I've got."

JENNIFER'S SELF-SURVEILLANCE	
Sensations	Rapid breathing. My face flushed.
Feelings	I feel like I can't say no.
Triggers	Jerod asked for money to go to a movie. And money has been really tight for me.
Thoughts	Jerod has had a rough life lately. He needs to have some fun. I hate to see him upset.
Schema	*No Control.* I can't say no to my kid.

Pam reviews Jennifer's Self-Surveillance chart. "Very nice start, Jennifer. You are obviously aware of your bodily sensations when you get upset. And you identified your trigger, thoughts, and schema quite accurately. Let me help you with the feeling category. Lots of people confuse thoughts and feelings. What you put under 'Feelings' actually belongs under 'Thoughts.' You can describe feelings in a single word. Words like sadness, fear, anger, joy, anxiety, embarrassment, pride, shame, guilt, disgust, love, hate, and exhilaration. What word best captures how you felt at the time?"

"That's easy—guilt. That's my middle name. I feel guilty I haven't been able to give Jerod the life he deserves. His dad and I divorced when he was small and as a single parent, I haven't been able to provide him with the extras his friends have."

"Okay, good. Let's put guilt down as the feeling. Oh, and you have some extra thoughts you can put down that you just told me. How about your adding 'I haven't been able to give Jerod the life he deserves' under the 'Thoughts' column? Later, we'll subject those thoughts and the schema to closer scrutiny, but for now let's look at your next Self-Surveillance."

JENNIFER'S SELF-SURVEILLANCE #2	
Sensations	Queasiness in my stomach. Tightness in my chest.
Feelings	Fear. I felt that Jerod was hurt or in trouble.
Trigger	Jerod stayed out until 3:00 A.M.
Thoughts	If something happened to Jerod, I couldn't go on. I love him so much. I would just die.
Schema	Anxious-Attachment. I worry about whether I could go on if anything happened to my child.

"Jennifer, this is really excellent work. Again, you seem very aware of the signals your body is giving you. That's good because those help alert you. You know that when your body reacts, important feelings and thoughts need to be looked at. And you knew what triggered your sensations, along with your thoughts. And I think you nailed the schema on the head. Your Anxious-Attachment causes you to assume the worst. You also accurately identified a feeling."

"Oops. I see I also put a thought under Feelings again. 'I felt that Jerod was hurt or in trouble,' should really be 'I thought that Jerod was hurt or in trouble.'"

"By God, I think she's got it!" Pam beams. "I see you have one more Self-Surveillance. How about we look at it?"

JENNIFER'S SELF-SURVEILLANCE	
Sensations	My heart was beating a thousand times a minute. My palms were sweaty.
Feelings	Jerod announced he was dropping out of school.
Trigger	Panic. I felt out of control. I also felt angry.
Thoughts	No one in my family ever dropped out of high school. He'll never amount to anything. What is he thinking? His life is ruined.
Schema	*Perfectionist.* I expect my child to hold the same high standards I have for myself.

"Okay. I need to move 'I felt out of control.' over to the Thoughts column." Jennifer sighs.

"That's true. But I wonder if you're feeling overwhelmed by what we're doing?"

"I don't really feel overwhelmed. I guess I'm impatient. And I'm feeling a little hopeless."

Now that you've seen how self-surveillance works, try this exercise on yourself.

SELF-SURVEILLANCE	
Sensations	
Feelings	
Triggers	
Thoughts	
Schema	

Changing What You Can and Accepting What You Can't

It's not unusual for parents to feel impatient and discouraged in the early going, as Jennifer did. It's tempting to think that you can make your kids do the right thing. Parents want to protect their children. They want their kids to live happily ever after. But life is not a fairy tale. And there is no fairy godmother, magic potion, or self-help book that will solve all of your kids' problems. Your task is to change what you can (i.e., your parenting) and accept what you can't. For example, let's say your child has a learning disability. You can arrange special tutoring and make sure the school does everything they can to help. But you can't ensure that your child will respond favorably to your efforts. Jennifer struggles with the issue of doing what she can, while accepting the limitations of her ability to ensure a favorable outcome for Jerod.

"Jennifer, you really seem to be understanding your triggers and schemas pretty well. That's a great start. Now that you're mastering this task, we're ready to go after these issues with a vengeance."

"But what am I going to do about Jerod? This is serious. He may really drop out of school. Knowing what triggers my Perfectionist schema won't change anything. How are we going to keep him in school? Pam, I'm really scared."

"I know you're scared Jennifer. You want what's best for Jerod, and dropping out of school isn't it. However, I think it's important to go over our goals again. We started with the premise that something was getting in the way of you parenting the way you wanted. Our job is to discover what that's about and to give you the ability to be the best parent you can be, no longer encumbered by emotional blocks. At this point, we've figured out a lot about why you parent the way you do. Would you agree?"

"Yeah sure, but nothing has changed for Jerod. He's what matters. I came here so I could help him."

"Actually, Jennifer, all we can do is change the way you parent. And doing that will help you feel better about yourself. Hopefully, Jerod will also do better as a result. But we can't guarantee or predict the future. Remember all the other influences in Jerod's life? No matter what we do to change your parenting, those influences will remain in place. He'll still have the same friends. He still has the same father. We can't change his genes."

"I'm sorry Pam. I don't mean to be so quarrelsome, but Jerod has been my life. I don't think I could stand to see him go down the tubes."

"Jennifer, have you ever encouraged Jerod to stay out late or drop out of school?"

"Of course not."

"Then you're not to blame if he does. You can't take the responsibility for how he turns out. You can't own it. All you can do now is be the best parent you can be. Somehow you'll have to find the strength to accept whatever happens. And that's really all any of us can do."

"I hear you, Pam. But I can't accept it. I'm not going to give up on Jerod."

"I'm not asking you to, Jennifer. But all I can offer you is help with how you parent. Together we can find the clouded windows through which you view Jerod and your world. And we can clean those up. Beyond that, what Jerod does with the rest of his life is out of our control. If you can accept that, we have some work to do. If you can't . . ."

Jennifer turns her head, looks out the window, silent. The condensation from Jennifer's glass of untouched ice water has left a ring on Pam's coffee table.

In Summary

In this chapter we have given you several tools for starting your own efforts to change. We told you to prepare for the up and down nature of change. Don't expect smooth, steady sailing. Perseverance eventually gets results.

Take your time with the Self-Surveillance exercise. It lays the foundation for changing your parenting. Doing this exercise will help you recognize the connections between sensations, feelings, triggers, thoughts, and schemas. Don't expect to master self-surveillance immediately. Continue to do it over a period of a few weeks. It will get easier and more helpful with practice.

Finally, remember that parents can learn to change themselves. Usually, those changes will help their kids, but not always. Focus on what you *can* change, not on what you can't.

Practice

Below, we provide you with another Self-Surveillance form. You may want to photocopy the form or draw your own in a notebook.

Self-Surveillance	
Sensations	
Feelings	
Trigger	
Thoughts	
Schema	

Chapter 6

CHANGING THINKING

Attacking Your Problematic Thoughts and Schemas

Dr. Douglas makes a practice of looking out at his clients before inviting them into his office. He notices Kenneth buried in a *Wall Street Journal*. Similarly, a book obscures Nick's face. He can only see Sally clearly, and she appears unnerved. Something's up.

"Sally, could you and Kenneth speak with me for a few minutes, and then I'll see Nick?"

Sally looks anxiously at Kenneth who fails to make eye contact. Kenneth carefully folds his newspaper and follows Sally into the office. Dr. Douglas feels the tension. He closes the door and takes a seat.

"What's up? You guys look pretty unhappy today."

Sally looks at Kenneth, who stares at the diplomas on the opposite wall. Uncomfortable with the prolonged silence, Sally responds, "The whole family fell apart this week. You know how we thought Nick was doing so great. Three failure notices from the school showed up in the mail. Apparently, he hasn't been turning in his assignments. We're stunned. Nick always excels at school. He's usually a straight-A student."

"I wish I could say I'm surprised, but I'm not," Dr. Douglas says. "I was pretty concerned last . . ."

"This is enough!" Kenneth lashes out, no longer able to contain himself. "You sit there like an omniscient soothsayer. The truth is, none of this would have happened if you hadn't stirred everyone in my family up. We have our problems, but now you've caused a mass rebellion. No one's listening to me anymore. Sally hotly contradicts everything I say, Lindsey's no better, and now Nick. I never had any trouble with Nick until we started this therapy thing. How do you respond to that, Dr. Douglas?"

"I don't blame you for being upset, Kenneth. I can see where the timing of all this makes it look like therapy is to blame. And maybe it is partly. For example, Sally's newfound assertiveness probably started with our therapy. Right now it sounds like Sally is arguing with you a little aggressively. We need to work on that."

Kenneth agrees, "Yes we do."

"What I'd like to propose is that we meet seven more times. First, with Nick by himself, in a few minutes. Then one family session, followed by two sessions with you, Kenneth, and two with Sally. Finally, we'll all meet together in a family session. If it doesn't feel like we're making good headway by then, let's quit. I know that's a lot to ask, but would you consider it?"

Kenneth doesn't answer right away.

Sally pleads, "Kenneth, we owe this to our family. Things were going bad before we came in here. Frankly, Kenneth, everyone was too afraid of you to talk about it."

"Afraid of me? Are you serious? Why?"

Tears in her eyes, Sally ventures on, "Kenneth, you don't realize how much your criticism hurts. Nobody can measure up to your standards. And you always have to tell us what to do, when to do it, and how to do it. It's your way or no way."

Dr. Douglas interrupts the discussion, "What you're discussing is important, Sally. But I need to move onto Nick in a minute. So let's get back to my question. Would both of you agree to seven more sessions?"

Sally nods in agreement immediately.

Kenneth clears his throat. "All right, seven more sessions. Then we evaluate. If things aren't considerably better by then, we stop therapy. Agreed?"

Dr. Douglas can't help but notice Kenneth's smile of contempt. Standing, he shakes Kenneth's hand, thereby accepting the challenge. Sally and Kenneth retreat to the waiting room as Dr. Douglas ushers Nick into his office.

"So, Nick, I gather things haven't been going so hot. Your parents told me about the school reports. What's going on?"

"Nothing."

"Oh. Well, I hear you've always done great in school. I have to wonder if something has been bothering you. Kids don't usually go from straight-A's to three failure notices for no reason."

"I just don't feel like doing the work anymore."

"What are you doing instead?"

"Hanging out in my room. At least it's quiet there."

"What's going on outside of your room that makes you go there for peace and quiet?"

"Everybody's mad. Mom and Dad are fighting and, of course, Lindsey's in the middle of it all. I just want to stay out of it. I hate fights. It makes me nervous."

"Sounds rough, Nick. Tell me, are you getting out and seeing your friends?"

"Not really. My dad never let's me stay out very long and it's hard to have anyone over. If my dad's home, he usually finds something to yell about. I used to play soccer, but I don't feel like doing that anymore."

"Why's that?"

"I feel tired. And I never play well enough to please my dad anyway."

"Are you sleeping okay?"

"I wake up in the middle of the night and can't go back to sleep."

"Are you eating the same as you always have?"

"Probably not. Nothing tastes good."

"Answer this. If zero represents as sad and down as you can imagine, and one hundred is as happy and up as you could be, how would you rate your mood lately from zero to one hundred?"

"I don't know. I guess about twenty."

"Do you ever think the world would be better off without you?"

"No. I'm not about to kill myself, if that's what you mean."

Dr. Douglas was glad to hear that response, but he also knew Nick was showing signs of depression. And it seemed as though much of Nick's depression related to the intense conflict in the family. Nick felt powerless. Dr. Douglas deemed a family session as a high priority.

On the afternoon of the family session, Kenneth arrives home early. Nick is in his room with the door closed, Lindsey is on the phone, and Sally is pulling out paper plates from the cupboard. Dirty dishes overflow the sink. The doorbell rings. Sally asks, "Kenneth, could you get that? And do you have twenty dollars for the pizza? I'll get the kids. We've got to leave in twenty minutes. Nick! Lindsey! Get in here. Hurry up. We've got to eat and go."

Kenneth puts the pizza on the table. He notices it's smothered with greasy pepperoni, sausage, Canadian bacon, and extra cheese. As usual, Sally didn't seem concerned about his high cholesterol. Lindsey arrives, still talking on the phone, and grabs a slice. Sally doesn't bother with a plate as she rushes to retrieve Nick from his room.

"Come on, Nick. We have to go."

Nick, finally coaxed from his room, searches for the smallest slice. "Mom. Dad. I don't have to go see Dr. Douglas. I made up all that school work. I even did extra credit. My grades are back on track. You don't have to worry about me anymore."

Sally replies, "Dr. Douglas wants everybody there. Please don't give us trouble about it."

Kenneth speaks for the first time, "I'm with you kid. This is a waste of time. But, a deal is a deal. Let's go."

In Dr. Douglas's waiting room Nick complains, "I have a stomachache. I'll just wait out here."

Kenneth, already annoyed about being there, looks disgusted. His voice rises, "Enough of that, Nick. You always complain about being sick. Toughen up, kid. How did you ever get to be such a wimp?"

Sally angrily lashes out, "For God's sakes, Kenneth, leave the boy alone! This is exactly why we're here. He doesn't need any more of your senseless attacks."

Lindsey puts her arm around Nick protectively. She glares at her father. "Mom's right, Dad. Nick doesn't have anything to do with this. Stop picking on him."

The sounds of the argument invade Dr. Douglas' quiet reflection. He sighs, alerted to the difficult session ahead. He may only have six sessions remaining to help this troubled family. With apprehension, he greets them in the waiting room.

Dr. Douglas has a couch and three chairs in his office. Kenneth immediately heads for the chair most removed from the others. Nick and Lindsey take the couch, and Sally takes a chair next to the couch, leaving an empty chair next to Kenneth. The family sits in silence.

"I'd like to start with defining the problems. Then, we'll deal with what's behind them and how to change it. The way we're going to do this is to brainstorm. Everyone will get a chance to talk. I want to set some ground rules. First of all, let's keep our voices down. Yelling won't help. Second, give each person the chance to finish. No interrupting. Finally, let's be respectful. No name-calling. If that sounds all right, who'd like to talk first?"

"I would," Sally declares. "I'm sick and tired of Kenneth's

unending contempt. All he does is find fault. There's never a positive word for anyone. No one is good enough. When he's home, we walk around on eggshells. Everyone is glad when he works late or travels."

Lindsey chips in, "That's true. Nick's got the right idea. He stays in his room by himself. I don't blame him. Sometimes I wish I could drop out of the family like he has."

Kenneth blurts out, "I knew it. You call this therapy? It's another ambush. Let's all get together and blame Kenneth."

"Well, Dad, it *is* your fault!" Lindsey exclaims.

"Who was out drinking and driving, young lady? And God knows what else you were doing. You're turning into a little slut." Kenneth feels his face flush as his anger surges.

"See, Kenneth, there you go again with your verbal abuse." Sally's anger erupts, "I'm sick of it! Kenneth, let me tell you, I'm about ready to give up on this marriage. I'm never happy anymore. You're angry and vicious."

"Hold on you two, I . . ." Dr. Douglas attempts to quell the turmoil.

Kenneth interrupts Dr. Douglas, deaf to his request. "Sally, if I'm vicious, you're so busy trying to be friends with the kids that you don't care how they turn out."

Dr. Douglas stands, "Time out. I'm not going to allow all of you to . . ."

A sob stops Dr. Douglas in midsentence. Everyone turns to see Nick cowering, doubled over, weeping. Barely lifting his head, he gasps, "Stop it. Everybody just stop it. I can't stand this. I don't want to be in this family anymore. Everyone hates each other. Families are supposed to be happy."

Lindsey turns to hug Nick. "Everything is going to be okay. We've always got each other."

Dr. Douglas, noticing Kenneth's changed demeanor, inquires, "Kenneth, I see tears in your eyes. What's that about?"

The kids and Sally turn toward Kenneth, surprised.

"I'm sorry, Nick. I'm sorry. I'm so sorry. This isn't what I want for my family. I . . . I love you. I love you all," he stammers. "I don't know how we got to this point. I want us to be happy, too. Maybe I have screwed up. Maybe it's really all my fault. All I've wanted is the best for you."

Lindsey, still holding on to Nick, leans toward her father when she sees him crying. "Oh, Daddy, don't let Mom leave. Please do something."

Kenneth wipes his tears and sadly replies, "I don't know, princess. It might be too late. I guess I've been a terrible husband

and father. I don't know what I can do. I've ruined everything. I don't blame everyone for hating me."

Dr. Douglas seizes the opportunity to form an alliance with Kenneth. "Just a second, Kenneth. I think you and everyone else need to step back and take a realistic look at your role in this family. Although I agree you criticize too much, I don't think you're responsible for all the woes of your family. Let's look at some of your positive contributions. First, you work hard to support the lifestyle of your family. I'm sure there have been many times when all the hours you've put in seem overwhelming. But every day, you go to work. You also protect your family. You installed burglar and fire alarm systems. You buy the safest cars. You try to keep your kids from danger. You have high standards for your kids. And there's nothing wrong with that. You are a model for teaching the value and importance of work. And you work hard to keep order in the family. Are these terrible qualities? I don't think so. You even agreed to come to therapy which is, I suspect, the last thing on earth you ever wanted to do."

Sally, eyes still red, shifts her defiant stance. "You're right, Dr. Douglas. I know how hard coming to therapy has been for Kenneth. And, in many ways, he's been a good husband and father. I lost my temper a minute ago. It's not like me. I'm sorry. I don't want to leave. I just want things to get better."

"Nothing is more important to me than my family. When Sally and I got married, I dreamed about the family we'd create. And in that dream, our family was happy. I vowed I would never treat my kids the way my father treated me. And yet, that's exactly what I did. I'll do whatever I need to do to make my family happy."

Dr. Douglas concludes the session by explaining self-surveillance as a way for Kenneth to start tracking the sensations, feelings, triggers, and thoughts associated with his problematic schemas. Kenneth agrees to complete at least four Self-Surveillance charts as a prelude to changing his thinking.

This chapter is about changing thinking. So far we've only shown you crisis and chaos. What do these have to do with change?

How do you change cream into butter? You shake it up. Research suggests that turmoil and upset often precede change. Kenneth and Sally's family had gone along for years covering up and avoiding problems. They needed to confront issues head on. That's painful and difficult. Meaningful change requires an honest appraisal. Sometimes such an appraisal causes a little chaos. Chaos is uncomfortable, but it may be necessary for getting change underway. Now we'll teach you to calm chaos.

Arguing The case

The following week Kenneth arrives for his individual appointment.

"Where's your suit and tie, Kenneth?" Dr. Douglas inquires with a smile.

"I took the afternoon off. Nick had a soccer game."

"I'm glad to hear Nick's back in soccer. So, how has the week gone?"

"Actually, a little better. I've been trying not to be so controlling. When I completed those Self-Surveillance charts, I found myself holding back. I realize I don't always have to be in charge. Sally's calmed down and so have the kids. Nick has started to pull up his grades. And I got him back into soccer. Of course, he didn't do so well in the game. The coach was terrible. It really pissed me off. I had to direct Nick's play from the sideline. A couple of times I yelled at Nick to pass the ball while the idiot coach told him to keep control of it. By the end of the game I'd lost my voice from so much screaming."

"Hmm, I am glad to hear you're working on that control issue. And it's great that your family is doing better. But sometimes schemas, being the core issues they are, creep up on us. I suspect your control schema crept up at the soccer game. What do you think?"

"Okay, I admit I was doing a little coaching from the sideline. But I had to do it. The coach was incompetent."

"So, you had to do this? What would have happened if you hadn't been there?"

"Well, I guess the game would have gone on without me. But Nick might not have done as well."

"And . . . ?"

"Oh. So your point is . . . your point is," Kenneth's voice drops, "I've done it again, haven't I?"

"Bingo. I've got a technique for dealing with this sort of thing, Kenneth. Of course, you have to keep up the self-surveillance because you aren't catching all of the important incidents yet. But let's take the soccer game as an example and I'll show you how to argue the case against your schema. As a lawyer, you'll be a natural. This technique is a logical way to change distorted thinking. Let me draw another chart."

ARGUING THE CASE			
Trigger	Schema	Thoughts and Arguments for:	Thoughts and Arguments against:

"Kenneth, you told me that the soccer coach was incompetent. Let's write that event down as the trigger. What schema did that evoke?"

"Obviously, I wanted to take charge of the game and make it turn out the way I wanted. I guess you would say that's my Excessive-Control schema."

"Right. Now, in the next column, let's list all the arguments and thoughts that run through your mind in support of your need to control this situation."

"Well, I thought I could do a better job of coaching. I also hated to see Nick not do as well as he could. The team would surely lose without better input."

"Good. Now, are there any arguments or thoughts that go against the need to control this situation? This is usually harder to do, but try to come up with a few counterarguments even if you don't believe them."

Kenneth thinks for a moment before responding, "I guess it could embarrass Nick when I shout from the sidelines. The coach probably doesn't like it either. How's that?"

"Good. Let's also look at the evidence. You said that your input makes a big difference. Does the team win more often when you attend the games and tell the kids what to do?"

"No. Come to think of it, the only game they won this year was when I wasn't there."

"And what about Nick. Does he play better when you coach him?"

"No, he claims I make him nervous. Maybe he's right."

"Bottom line then, does the evidence support your thoughts that the team and Nick play better with your guidance?"

"You're good. I get the point. No, they don't play better."

"And there's more. Tell me what the worst possible outcome

would be if your schema didn't take over. What would have happened in this game if you had just watched?"

"Pretty much what did happen. Except that no one would have been embarrassed."

"That's basically true, Kenneth. But still, what would be the worst imaginable outcome of letting go of control?"

"Well, they lost, but I suppose they might have done even worse. And Nick might not have played as well. When I think about it, though, I'm not sure that's true. Nick seemed confused out there when the coach and I gave him different instructions."

"That's a good point. But let's assume the worst did occur. The team lost by ten points and Nick looked horrible out on the field. How awful would that have been?"

"So what you're getting at is that this is not an Olympic competition. If they lose, it's not the end of the world. And if Nick plays poorly, life will go on. But I act like it won't."

"You got it. Let's take a look at what we've got."

ARGUING THE CASE			
Trigger	Schema	Thoughts and Arguments for:	Thoughts and Arguments against:
The way the coach was directing the team.	*Excessive-Control*	I can do better than the coach. I hate to see Nick do poorly. The team will lose without my input.	I embarrass Nick. I irritate the coach. The evidence says that Nick and the team don't play one wit better when I'm yelling from the sidelines. The worst thing that could happen is the team and Nick will play more poorly. And that's not so bad.

"You know, Dr. Douglas, this kind of logic makes sense to me. I didn't realize that therapy was like this. I really like what you are doing. And I'm beginning to change the way I think about this issue. Thanks."

"You're doing all the work, Kenneth. Now how about we take a look at one of your Self-Surveillance assignments and use the situation for another round of arguing the case?"

"Sure. Here's one I did last week."

KENNETH'S SELF-SURVEILLANCE #2	
Sensations	Tightness in my shoulders and neck.
Feelings	Fear and worry.
Trigger	Lindsey asked to spend the night at a girlfriend's house.
Thoughts	She's probably lying. She'll go out and get into more trouble. She'll probably drink and have boys over. She could get pregnant and ruin her life.
Schema	Distrust

"Excellent. You nailed it. Most people struggle a little with this exercise. Often they confuse feelings and thoughts, but you were able to clearly differentiate between the two. By the way, how did you respond to her request?"

"I let her go because I'm trying to work on both my Distrust and Excessive-Control schemas. But I felt terrible. I couldn't sleep all night."

"That must have been difficult. But, I have to congratulate you for taking that step. Now, let's examine it further. You already have identified the schema, its trigger, and some of the thoughts that accompany it. Now, let's 'argue the case.' Let's take the thoughts you already put down and add any arguments you can think of to support your Distrust schema."

"She's probably lying because she lied in the past. When she got into trouble the last time, it involved drinking and boys. Kids can't be trusted nowadays. Who knows if that girl's parents are even going to be home?"

"Good. How about thoughts and arguments that counter your Distrust schema?"

"All right. Overall, Lindsey has a very good track record for telling the truth. Since that incident she's expressed considerable remorse. And she's done everything I've asked of her. It's unlikely Lindsey would get pregnant. Her mother and I believe in educating our children about those matters. Lindsey plans to go to college and I know she doesn't want a pregnancy to interfere with her plans. Some kids can be trusted. I've known Lindsey's friend and her parents for several years and there's no good reason to think they would let the kids go unsupervised."

"You're getting pretty good at this. Your law school training is paying off. One more question. Let's just say Lindsey was unsupervised, there were boys, and she got pregnant. How would you deal with that? Would it forever ruin her life?"

"Yes. That would be horrible."

"Horrible, yes. But could you deal with it?"

"Wow. I don't know. I guess there are several difficult options. We'd have to talk about it and decide what to do. It sure wouldn't be easy."

"No, it wouldn't. But would it have to forever ruin her life?"

"No, I suppose it wouldn't. It would be formidable, but with the help and support of her family, she could deal with it. It wouldn't have to ruin her life."

"That's right. So, here's your case."

ARGUING THE CASE #1			
Trigger	Schema	Thoughts and Arguments for:	Thoughts and Arguments against:
Lindsey asked to spend the night at a friend's house.	Distrust	Lindsey has lied in the past. She drank underage. Kids can't be trusted. The parents might not supervise the kids. Boys might come over and she could get pregnant.	As far as I know, Lindsey only lied once. She expressed remorse. She generally behaves. She knows how not to get pregnant and she doesn't want to get pregnant. I know the girl's family and they aren't the type to leave kids unsupervised. If she did get pregnant, we could deal with it.

Kenneth nods his head slowly, "Looking over this case, I'm really glad I let her go. But what about the way I felt, so worried and anxious?"

"That's your schema trying to maintain control, Kenneth. You're doing the right work and taking the right actions. Your feelings will shift with time. Do you remember the first time you ever rode a bike without training wheels? Most of us are scared to death, but the fear diminishes each time you ride. With practice, the fear goes away."

"So what you're saying is that I'm afraid to give up my schemas and with practice my fear will dissipate?"

"That's exactly what I'm saying, Kenneth. Now let's look at one more Self-Surveillance so we can Argue the Case."

"Okay, here's an interesting one. Sally and I got into an argument about Nick's homework. I wanted him to recopy it because his handwriting was virtually illegible. Sally said he needed to go to bed and he'd already worked hard that night. Here's my Self-Surveillance."

Kenneth's Self-Surveillance #2	
Sensations	Nothing really clear. Just a sense of uneasiness. Maybe a slight pressure in my chest.
Feelings	Irritated. Annoyed.
Trigger	Sally told Nick he'd done enough on his homework, when it clearly needed to be rewritten.
Thoughts	Sally is giving Nick permission to have sloppy standards. How's he ever going to get into a top college that way?
Schema	Perfectionist

"Okay, Kenneth. Now let's go over the argument for your case."

		ARGUING THE CASE	
Trigger	**Schema**	**Thoughts and Arguments for:**	**Thoughts and Arguments against:**
Sally tells Nick he's done enough on his home-work when I think he hasn't.	Perfectionist	Nick won't have high standards if we don't expect them of him. He won't get into a good college. He'll never get anywhere in life. He'll be lazy.	No one needs to work as hard as I do. Nick almost always excels in school. His test scores suggest he can go to school just about any-where he wants. Nick has never been lazy.

"That's terrific, Kenneth. One more question. I'm wondering, what if Nick doesn't get into a great college? And what if he ends up going to a vocational school? Or worse yet, what if he works at a fast-food restaurant when he graduates from high school and doesn't go to college at all?"

"Now come on, that's not going to happen."

"Quite unlikely, true. But I think it's important to face the worst possible outcome of your fears. Will Nick not getting into the right college necessarily ruin his life?"

"All right. Yes, of course, it's possible to be successful without a college degree. And money isn't everything. I suppose there are a few people who live happy lives working at fast-food restaurants. Not my first choice for Nick. But ultimately, it's really up to Nick, isn't it? He could work his way up in the fast-food industry or not even do that if he chooses. I've given him a good start and what he makes of it is up to him."

"Is this Kenneth I'm talking to? You sound like a different person."

"I'm starting to feel like a different person."

"Speaking of feelings, when you drop your perfectionist attitude about Nick, how do you feel?"

"Relieved. It helps. I'm not as stressed about it. I feel calmer."

"That's what I was talking about earlier. Changing your thinking changes your feelings."

"Arguing the case" is an excellent way of challenging the thinking generated by your problematic schemas. It is one of the most important exercises in the book. The column labeled, "Thoughts and Arguments against" often generates the most difficulty. Why? Because schemas work hard to survive. As we said before, schemas distort thinking. They make you envision dire consequences if you fail to believe in them. For example, Kenneth truly believed it was imperative for Nick to rewrite his homework. His Perfectionist schema caused him to exaggerate the importance of every assignment. At some level, he believed lowering his standards, even slightly, would endanger Nick's entire future. When schemas take hold, they act like blinders. Schemas keep you from seeing or even considering evidence that could contradict them.

Therefore, it's a good idea to spend some time completing this column. First, come up with whatever you can on your own. Then, you might want to ask for input from a trusted friend or partner. Finally, answer the following list of questions. The answers to these questions might not come to you immediately. Take time to think them over:

- What is the evidence that contradicts your "Thoughts and Arguments for"? In other words, have those thoughts always been true? Do you have experiences that contradict them?

- How could your schema and its associated thoughts cause trouble for your family?

- How could your schema and its associated thoughts cause you to do the wrong thing?

- If your best friend had this schema, would you look at his or her thoughts differently than you do when you have them?

- What evidence do you have that your "Thoughts and Arguments for" are not completely 100 percent accurate?

- What is the worst possible outcome of your "Thoughts and Arguments for?" How likely is that outcome? Could you cope with it if it did occur?

The Split-Chair Strategy

Six-thirty always comes too early for Jennifer. The soothing sounds of her favorite jazz station do little to ease the transition from sleep to wakefulness. Jennifer's energy reserve has been exhausted. Wearily, with no enthusiasm for the day ahead, she rolls out of bed and makes her way to the bathroom. Damp towels litter the floor. And as usual, the raised toilet seat reflect Jerod's presence in her house. She rinses cigarette ashes from the sink before washing her face. Never before has her home been in such disarray. She simultaneously feels despondent at her own inertia and furious at Jerod.

Jennifer finishes dressing. Lately she has paid little attention to her appearance. She listlessly gathers her purse and work calendar and heads downstairs. A gasp of frustration escapes from her when she sees her son. "Damn it, Jerod. You're going to burn the house down."

Jerod, still asleep, sprawled on the couch, doesn't move. A half-smoked cigarette lies in an ashtray full of butts. Several cans of soda lay strewn about the floor. The television obviously was never turned off. Jerod hasn't attended school since he got off probation a week ago. All of Jennifer's pleading has gone unheeded. Hopeless and defeated, Jennifer collapses into a chair and cries. Jerod lifts his head, "Not again, Mom. Just leave me alone. You make such a big deal out of everything."

"Big deal? You're not going to school. You don't have a job. You sleep until noon every day and don't do anything to help me around the house. That's not a big deal?"

"Whatever. If it bothers you, I'll go upstairs and sleep in my room."

"Maybe Pam was right. Since I quit seeing her, I've tried for six months and clearly I can't change you. But I can learn to deal with what happens to you. And I don't have to put up with this."

"Yeah, right. I'll see you later. Do what you have to do," Jerod dares as he trudges upstairs to his room.

Once again, Jennifer draws on her inner strength and decides she needs help. She realizes she has done as much as she can with Jerod. It hasn't worked. She wonders if she should have quit therapy so abruptly. She swallows her pride and calls Pam for an appointment.

When Jennifer arrives for her appointment, Pam immediately notices the change in her appearance. "I'm glad to see you again, Jennifer. But I'm sorry to hear you're having such a rough time. Why don't you tell me more about it?"

"Last time I was here, I walked out thinking you were wrong—that there *was* something I could do to change Jerod. After six months of fighting, begging, and bribing, I see that's not true. I can't change him. But I do need to figure out what to do with him. He's worn me down. I feel depressed. I've neglected the few friends I made last year. I'm so tired of this. Jerod sits around doing nothing all day long. He contributes nothing. He'll be eighteen in a couple of weeks and he's going nowhere."

"Well, Jennifer, I don't mean to be harsh, but why should he? You're giving him food and shelter. A free ride."

"What else can I do? If I kick him out, he'll be homeless. I don't want to abandon him like I did before. Anyway, his father won't take him."

"Jennifer, this isn't like before. He's almost eighteen years old now. He'll be considered an adult in two weeks. Do you think it might be time to finally set limits on Jerod?"

"Oh God, Pam, it's so hard for me to do this. I just don't know if I can."

"How about we try an experiment? It's called the Split-Chair Strategy. You remember what schemas are, don't you?"

"Yes. And I remember which ones I have. I have Anxious-Attachment, Blameworthy, Perfectionist, and No Control. I can't say no to Jerod."

"You have a good memory. Let's work on the No Control schema. See these two chairs facing each other? I'd like for you to sit in one of them and immerse yourself in the No Control schema. I want you to imagine that No Control is the absolute and total reality for you. In other words, you can't say no to Jerod; if you do make rules, you can't enforce them. Pretend like you're talking to another part of yourself. Use the pronoun 'you' as though that part of you is actually sitting in the other chair."

"That's easy, that is my reality."

"Usually it is, Jennifer. But I think you have at least a small part of you that understands the value of saying no. I want you to put that part of yourself in the other chair. Start out by sitting in the 'No Control' chair and tell the imagined other part of you all the reasons you shouldn't and can't say no to Jerod. Once you run out of arguments, switch to the other chair. Pretend you believe that saying no and setting limits is crucial. You don't have to believe it, but try to convince the 'No Control Jennifer' you are right."

"I'm going to feel pretty silly talking to an empty chair."

"I know. But give it a shot."

"All right, this is the 'No Control Jennifer.' Jennifer, you

can't say no to Jerod. Look at the life he's had. Poor kid. His
father left when he was little. You can't afford to buy him the
kind of clothes all of his friends wear. He's almost eighteen and
he doesn't have a car. If you say no, you'll hurt him even more.
You feel terrible when you say no to him. You can't ask me to do
that . . . I can't think of anything else."

"Okay, take the other chair and try to argue with the 'No
Control Jennifer.'"

Jennifer takes the other chair and surprises herself by saying,
"You know, Jennifer, you sound pathetic. Jerod's life wasn't that
bad. He was never hungry or cold. He had enough clothes. And
why are you even thinking about trying to buy him a car? Are
you crazy? Saying no to him is probably the best thing you could
ever do for him."

"Outstanding, Jennifer," Pam supports her. "Now, take the
other chair again and argue as the 'No Control Jennifer.'"

"Okay. What kind of mother would hurt her own child?
And Jerod needs a car. How will he ever get a job without a car?
He's a fragile kid. If you're too hard on him, he'll fall apart."

Pam interrupts, "Good, now switch chairs again."

"Maybe he needs to fall apart if he's ever going to grow up.
And he could get a job that he could walk to. Eventually he could
buy his own car like most people do."

"Good, switch again," Pam instructs.

"If you say no, he'll hate you. He might get so mad he'll
never speak to you again. You might never see him again. You
couldn't stand that."

Pam breaks in, "You're doing a great job, Jennifer. Let me
point out something that happened. I think another schema is
rearing its head. And this schema may be the toughest one for
you to stand up against. I think it even supports the No Control
schema. Do you know which one it is?"

"I was just talking about never seeing Jerod again. That felt
really bad. I guess that's got to be my greatest fear. It must be
because of my Anxious-Attachment schema."

"Correct. So let's change schemas in midstream. Instead of
No Control, argue in favor of Anxious-Attachment in the first
chair and against it in the other chair. This may be harder to do."

"Well, like I started to say before, I'm—I mean, *you're*—
afraid that Jerod will hate you if you stand up to him. He's your
whole life. Without Jerod, your life would be meaningless."

Pam signals for Jennifer to switch chairs.

"Let's see, now I'm the reasonable Jennifer who does not
have the Anxious-Attachment schema. Okay, Jerod will probably

not hate you if you stand up to him. He might get very mad and not speak to you for a while, but kids don't just stop loving their parents. You focus too much of your life around him anyway. It's time for you to make more friends and maybe even start dating again. It's time to get a life. You wouldn't like it if he never spoke to you again. You'd hate it, but you'd live. This is something you have to do for both him and yourself."

"Switch again," Pam suggests.

"Oh, this side is much easier. I—no, I mean *you*—have no life without Jerod. You're too old to make friends and start dating. He's all you have. He needs you. You can't abandon him."

Jennifer switches chairs without Pam's encouragement. "No, you do have a life without Jerod. You're only thirty-eight for heaven's sake. There is a woman in your office that's fifty-two who just got engaged. And she dated four men in the last few years. And you've been wanting to go back for your master's degree for a long time. Why not now? It's not good for a grown woman to focus her life on her nearly adult son. You both need more space."

Pam cuts off the exercise. "Jennifer, how are you feeling right now?"

"You know, I'm beginning to sense a shift in my thinking. I feel a little bit stronger. It's funny, this exercise seemed kind of silly and artificial at first. But I really feel something happening. I realize I do need to set some limits with Jerod. And I have to figure out what those will be. And I have to be prepared for whatever reaction he has, including his anger and rejection. I have to focus on developing a more meaningful life for myself. Maybe I will look into taking a couple of classes. Thank you."

"You did a great job with this exercise, Jennifer. And you should pat yourself on the back for having the courage to come back to therapy and do battle with these issues again. Changing the thinking that supports schemas is very hard. The work isn't complete. Now that your thinking has started to change, we can make plans for how to keep these changes up so that you can parent like you want."

In Summary

Chaos and turmoil introduced this chapter. Kenneth's family seemed to be falling apart. Don't be surprised if your own efforts to change your parenting result in a temporary increase in family discord. And don't let discord discourage your further attempts at change. Remember, sometimes things have to get worse before they get better.

We then presented two techniques for changing thinking. The first of these was called Arguing the Case. You can employ this strategy for every problematic parenting schema you have. Use it again and again, every time your schema is triggered. Each time you complete the exercise you guarantee that the next time will be easier. And it will be easier to accomplish every other task we suggest.

Practice

The second technique, the Split-Chair Strategy, seems pretty odd at first. We think you'll be surprised by how well it works. Lock your doors, pull down the curtains, unplug your phone, and do it. It won't work if you try to do it in your head. Literally talk out loud, just like Jennifer did. It's the only way to get the issues out of your head and into the open. Remember, schemas thrive in the dark.

More Practice

Go back to one of your Self-Surveillance forms and put the "trigger" and the "schema" into the first two columns of the Arguing the Case form below. Then, put your thoughts and arguments that favor the schema into the next column. Finally, make your case against the schema. Use the questions provided earlier in this chapter to help you develop answers for the Thoughts and Arguments against column.

ARGUING THE CASE			
Trigger	Schema	Thoughts and Arguments for:	Thoughts and Arguments against:

Chapter 7

THE MIDDLE WAY
OF PARENTING

The Path to Calming Chaos

Agitators

The halls are crowded with children moving onto their next class. As Dr. Chavez navigates the way to his office, several second-graders pull on his jacket. "Can we come and see you? Do we have group today?"

Patting one of the kids on the shoulder, Dr. Chavez replies, "Not now, Amber, I have another appointment. But I'll visit your class this afternoon for group. Do you remember what we're going to talk about?"

"You're going to teach us about how to get along on the playground. And I want to talk to you about this fifth grade boy who's always picking on us."

Dr. Chavez instinctively knows who that fifth grade boy is. And his mother happens to be his next appointment. When he arrives at his office, he's surprised to find Debra a few minutes early. "Debra, nice to see you." Dr. Chavez reaches out his hand to greet her.

"I'm sorry it's been a few weeks since we've met. My husband was out of town and I got really busy."

"Well, come on in and let's talk about what's been going on." Debra and Dr. Chavez enter the office and sit down before Dr. Chavez says, "Remember last time we talked about trying to take an honest look at Quinton's behavior. How's that been going?"

"It's almost like you took the blinders off me, Dr. Chavez. You were right. And so was the school. Quinton's awful. He never listens. He always talks back. He's constantly teasing the neighborhood kids even though I told him not to. He's a total brat."

"Can you give me a specific example of Quinton's misbehavior? Like tell me something that happened in the last couple of days."

"Every time I tell him to do something, he acts like I'm invisible. Even when I scream my lungs out at him, he laughs in my face." Debra's face tightens and her speech quickens, "He really makes my blood boil. I get furious."

"Does your anger help control him?"

"No, when I yell at him, he always yells right back at me."

"Give me a specific example of a conflict."

"It's all the time. He's not a baby, he's in fifth grade. He should know better. He doesn't do anything right. Honestly, Dr. Chavez, I'm not even sure I like my own kid. What else can I say?"

"Debra, as hard as it is on you, I am glad you are letting yourself see some of the problems. That's an important step. Parenting is all about balance. It's finding the Middle Way. When I listen to you talk, I hear words like always, never, constant, should, brat, and total. I call words like those 'agitators.' Agitators set people off. They provoke. They are extreme and when people use these words, they react excessively. Anger, as I think you sense, doesn't help control behavior, and anger distances you from the Middle Way. Are you following me?"

"Not really. Quinton is totally out of control. I'm afraid he's really a bad kid."

"Right now, you do see him as totally out of control. You flipped from seeing Quinton as Blameless and now you see him as Blameworthy. Your schema is still giving you trouble. While it's true that Quinton misbehaves a lot, if we look hard enough, we can probably catch him behaving. Let me tell you about the three types of agitators and then we can look at how they cause distortions and overreactions. I call the first category of agitators 'extremist language.' This includes words like always, ceaseless, never, every time, forever, unending, and total. There are few absolutes in this world. For instance, you told me that Quinton never listens. Can you possibly remember one time when he did listen to you?"

"I suppose so. He usually comes to dinner when I tell him.

And since he's been in fifth grade, I never have to tell him to comb his hair. My God, he spends more time on his hair than I do. And I guess he gets ready for school when I tell him it's time."

"Good. Realizing that give us something to build on. When you use extremist language, it feels hopeless. And it makes you mad. Can you agree, then, that it isn't really true Quinton *never* listens?"

"Okay. But he doesn't listen much of the time."

"True. But when we acknowledge he does listen some of the time, we can look for those instances and reward him. As I said, we can build on successes. Instead of saying, 'Quinton never listens,' try saying, 'Quinton doesn't listen as much as I'd like,' and see how it feels."

"Really? Say it?"

"Yes. Really say it."

"Okay. Quinton doesn't listen as much as I like. . . . Well, I guess that doesn't feel quite as bad. Do you mean to say that if I say this when Quinton isn't listening, I'm not going to get as mad at him?"

"Yes, actually. I think much of the time, you won't. I know it sounds far-fetched, but how we describe things in our minds affects the way we feel. Whenever you can, try to avoid using extreme language. And if you find yourself getting angry, check out what you're saying to yourself. Do you think you could try that out?"

"Sure. By the way, do you do husband training? He's always—oops, I mean, he often uses extremist language both with me and Quinton."

"Good catch on your language, Debra. Actually, as you know, I've invited him to our sessions. It's too bad that he feels he can't get away from work. For now, let's go onto the second category of agitators called judgmental language. It consists of words like should, must, and ought. These words also lead to anger and excessive disapproval. When you said, 'Quinton should know better,' you probably felt indignant. If instead, you had said, 'I would like for Quinton to know better,' does it feel a little less judgmental?"

"So you're saying that if I change the way I talk, I'm really going to feel differently?"

"I think with practice you will. It's one of the crucial steps toward finding the Middle Way of Parenting. So, let's look at the final category of agitators—labeling. Labeling includes words like bad kid, brat, monster, no good—you get the idea. These are sweeping, pejorative generalizations. Again, they lead to excessive reactions. And they don't help. Try to separate the person from the behavior. You can dislike some of Quinton's behavior, but if you call him a bad boy, he'll begin to believe it and act accordingly. When you are upset with him, single out the specific thing he did. Try not to label him. And I think, Debra, earlier when you told me that you didn't like Quinton, that was a result of you labeling him. Quinton isn't a bad boy. He's a boy who does a few too many bad things. When we label people bad, we tend to give up on them."

"You're right. I must admit, over the past few weeks, I've felt like shipping Quinton off to a military academy. I think I was starting to give up on him too early."

"I'm glad you can see that, Debra. Let me give you this chart of common agitators. It can help you stay on the lookout for destructive language in the way you talk to Quinton as well as the way you think about him."

AGITATORS		
Extremist Language	**Judgmental Language**	**Labeling**
always	should	bad
never	ought	brat
constant	must	monster
ceaseless		stupid
never ending		idiot
forever		awful
total		horrible

Dr. Chavez gives Debra the chart and says, "Look out for those words when you are thinking about Quinton and his behavior. Try to substitute more accurate words, and words that simply describe his behavior. And also watch for judgmental language and labeling. Next week, we'll talk about how that goes and move on to another technique."

Learning about agitators starts you on the path toward the Middle Way of Parenting. Agitators cue you to the possibility of an extreme schema at work. If you remember, in chapter 2, we told you extreme schemas lead to extreme moods, disregard contradictory evidence, put stress on relationships, create negative outcomes in children, and cause rigidity. Agitators help them do all of that. If you eliminate agitators from your regular vocabulary, you make it harder for extreme schemas to take control of your parenting. Now let's see how Debra is doing with Quinton at home.

"Quinton, it's time to do your homework."

No answer.

"Quinton, honey, it's time to do your homework."

No answer.

Voice rises, "Quinton, it's time *right now* to do your homework!"

Quinton doesn't flinch. He remains immersed in his video game.

Debra, losing patience, yanks the video game from his hand, and screams, "I am totally sick of you never listening to me . . . um, I mean, I really don't like it when you don't listen to me, honey."

Quinton looks at his mother for the first time since she spoke. "I'm in the middle of my game. I'll do my homework in a little while."

"I gave you a little while over an hour ago. A little while never comes for you, you brat!"

"I don't have to do what you say. I'm playing my game. Anyway, you're the one who said homework was stupid." Quinton's rising voice matches his mother's.

"Um, I mean . . . um . . . okay . . . let's see, geez, what am I supposed to say?"

"Gosh, I don't know, Mom. What are you talking about?" Quinton says, perplexed.

"Um, nothing, what I meant to say is: I'd really like you to do your homework now. I would prefer that, yes, that's it, it would please me if you would do your homework now. Hey, I think I got it."

Quinton, now really confused, answers, "What's wrong with you, Mom? If you promise to quit talking that way, I'll do my homework."

What we have tried to illustrate is how your first attempts at catching agitators might go. It may feel awkward at first. It will take you a while for it to become a habit. But your new language will help you avoid escalations of conflict. Your child may not always obey and you may have to deliver a consequence for misbehavior. However, you won't find yourself yelling and screaming. You'll be able to clearly speak to your child, without unnecessary harshness. When you dance an angry dance, your child will quickly follow your lead.

Schema Flash Cards

Glancing at his watch, Dr. Chavez reflects that Debra has not missed a session in the last three weeks. He hopes she continues with the progress she has made. Quinton has started to improve both at home and in school, though the changes are fragile at this point.

When she arrives, he asks, "So, Debra, how are you doing? We've seen a little progress at school, how about at home?"

"Actually, it felt pretty weird at first, but I'm getting the knack of eliminating those agitators. And, I've been tracking my schemas with the Self-Surveillance charts. You know, Quinton seems to be listening to me a little better. I almost like the kid again."

"That's great, Debra. Did anything happen this week that's really important for us to talk about?"

"Well, Quinton wasn't all that bad. For me, I'm finding I can easily identify and track my schemas. But, I don't always know what to do about them."

"Perfect. We're ready for the next technique. You know how kids learn their multiplication tables? They use flash cards. And that's the name of this strategy—schema flash cards. Tell me the three schemas that cause you the most trouble."

"That's easy. No Control, Blameless, and Blameworthy—I flip between those and Avoidant-Attachment."

"Let's start with No Control. First, tell me how you've defined No Control for yourself, and I'll write it on this flash card."

"For me, No Control means I hate to discipline Quinton. I find it very hard to say no, although I must say, it's been a little easier lately. But, if I had my choice, I wouldn't have anything to do with discipline."

"Okay. Good. Now, tell me what feelings and sensations you get when this schema is active. You've probably already written that on your Self-Surveillance chart."

"Yes, I have. I feel anxious. I feel tightness in my chest. It's hard to breathe."

"We talked about your childhood. Reflecting back, what do you think might have caused you to develop a No Control problem with your kids?"

"I've thought quite a bit about that, Dr. Chavez. My parents weren't particularly mean to me. I mean they didn't boss me around. They sort of left me alone. But I was so miserable. I was such a miserable child. I think I didn't want Quinton to be as unhappy as I was. I mistakenly thought that letting him do what he wanted would make him happier. After all, when I did attempt to set limits with Quinton, he cried."

"That's very insightful, Debra. Many people don't understand the connection between their own unhappiness and their tendency to spoil their kids. Now, I guess we know what the current triggers for your schema are: Quinton, Quinton, and Quinton."

"You're right. I don't know why, but he really pushes my buttons. I think maybe I've also felt guilty about the time in the hospital when he had a seizure."

"We'll keep that in mind. Now let's talk a little about the Middle Way of Parenting. The Middle Way lies between schema opposites. It integrates the opposites in a way that creates a better balance. So what would the Middle Way look like between No Control and Excessive-Control?"

"I suppose it would be moderate or appropriate control. In other words, I would let go of little, unimportant stuff. After all, kids need to have some freedom to make mistakes. That's the way they learn. But, it would also mean that I would enforce important rules that have to do with safety, health, or his overall well-being. And sometimes, enforce rules simply because I'm the adult and know what's best."

"Wow. That's excellent. Now, can you tell me a couple of specific actions you can take to carry that out?"

"What do you mean?"

"When you realize your schema has been triggered, what can you do to defuse it?"

"I can look over my cost/benefit analysis as a reminder that I need to change. And I can take a little time to reflect before I act. Maybe take some deep breaths like you showed me."

"And how about giving me two rules you really want to enforce with Quinton."

"All right. I have come to believe his homework is important. Even when it looks like busy work, I know that doing homework is a good habit. It will pay off for him in the future. And I want him to stop leaving stuff all over the living room."

"Good. Now, I have to tell you, you may need help on knowing exactly how to enforce those rules. We'll talk about that further next week. I have one other question for you. What happens when you fail to carry out your intentions with Quinton?

In other words, what will do you do when your schema gets the best of you?"

"Lately, I've been pretty hard on myself when I screw up. It's bad enough that Quinton's a screwup. When I am too, it's really horrible."

"That's what I was afraid of. You're getting so much better with Quinton. Now we have to teach you to lighten up on yourself. Look at all those agitators you just used against yourself. You used to have a hard time accepting blame and now you are overdoing it. I want you to accept responsibility, but with self-acceptance. So what's something better you can say to yourself when you slip? Something better than, 'I'm a screwup and it's really horrible.'"

Debra smiles. "I didn't realize I was doing that. I guess I could say, 'I don't like it when I make a mistake, but I'm only human. Mistakes happen.'"

"That's more like it. Now let me show you the card I've filled out. I'm going to ask you to carry it with you and read it at least once a day for a while. Also take it out and read it whenever you think you may have slipped up. Read it carefully and think about each part."

DEBRA'S *NO CONTROL* FLASH CARD

Schema Definition: I hate to discipline my kid. I find it very hard to say no. If I had my choice, I wouldn't have anything to do with discipline.

Feelings and Sensations: Anxious. Tightness in my chest. Hard to breathe.

Beginnings: I was miserable as a child. Quinton in the hospital—I felt guilty.

Current Triggers: Whenever Quinton talks back, doesn't listen, or disobeys.

The *Middle Way*: Moderate or appropriate control. Rules about safety, health, and overall well-being enforced.

Action Steps:

1. Look over cost/benefit analysis.

2. Take time to think before I act. Take a few deep breaths.

3. Enforce rules about leaving stuff all over the living room.

4. Make sure he does his homework.

Self-forgiveness: I don't like it when I make a mistake, but I'm only human. Mistakes happen.

Debra frowns, "That's nice. But, really, what will this flash card do for me? It looks kind of silly."

"That's what I thought the first time I looked at the flash card idea. However, I tried them out with both kids and their parents. I was surprised to find how useful people find them. Even carrying them in your pocket serves as a tangible reminder of the work you're doing. But why don't you try using flash cards for a couple of weeks and see? If you don't find them useful, we'll try something else."

Debra agrees. They proceed to fill out two more flash cards:

DEBRA'S *BLAMELESS/BLAMEWORTHY* FLASH CARD

Schema Definition: I hate admitting I made a mistake. When I can't deny I made a mistake, I beat myself up. I have the same reaction to Quinton. I either excuse his behavior or scream at him.

Feelings and Sensations: Angry. I feel hot and flushed.

Beginnings: I was teased as a child about my mother. There was no one to defend me.

Beginnings: When either Quinton or I make a mistake or are blamed for something.

The *Middle Way*: I will try to own up to mistakes and shortcomings on my part as well as Quinton's. We both need to accept responsibility without excessive blame.

Action Steps:

1. Look over cost/benefit analysis.

2. Take time to think before I act. Take a few deep breaths.

3. When I hear criticism, I will make myself listen to it seriously. It's probably at least partly true.

4. I will try to avoid using agitators with myself and Quinton.

Self-forgiveness: Everyone makes mistakes. I can learn from mistakes. There's no need to engage in what Dr. Chavez calls self-abuse.

DEBRA'S *AVOIDANT-ATTACHMENT* FLASH CARD

Schema Definition: I'm uncomfortable with hugging and kissing my kid. I don't know how to talk to him. I haven't said "I love you" since they were little.

Feelings and Sensations: Anxious. Detached. Phony.

Beginnings: Neither of my parents ever really talked to me. My dad was a little weird about touching—he made me feel uncomfortable. My mom was so depressed she never gave me any affection.

Current Triggers: When I put my kid to bed, I know I should hug him, but I pull back. When I am around other families and I see how close they are, I feel empty.

The *Middle Way*: I want to start hugging and kissing him good night. I also want to spend more time talking with him. I want my whole family to be closer.

Action Steps:

1. I will hug Quinton every day.

2. I will kiss Quinton good night.

3. I will learn about the activities that interest Quinton so I can talk with him about that (like video games for Quinton).

4. In the future I will get therapy for myself to learn more about my problems with intimacy. I might also get marital therapy at some point.

Self-forgiveness: This is a hard one for me. Of course it will take time to feel natural. I need to go slow with it because I didn't learn it as a child.

Flash Card Action Steps

You, like Debra, might think flash cards seem a little silly. After all, flash cards are usually reserved for school children. You may not know that many adults rely on them heavily for challenging tasks such as studying for advanced degrees, as well as the bar exam, medical licensure, the certified public accounting exam, and psychology licensure. Flash cards can help cement new learning. You might think the new learning involved with changing schemas isn't that complex. Intellectually, it probably isn't, but as we said before, schemas are stubborn. Defeating them presents a daunting emotional assignment. Flash cards give you a boost when schemas start to get the best of you.

Another advantage of the flash card strategy is that most of the information you've been learning gets organized on one small card. Having this in your pocket or purse makes it possible for you to review your learning whenever you need to. You have already completed most of the learning needed to fill out your own personal flash cards. The only step we haven't covered yet are the action steps. Action steps essentially are concrete plans or goals for making changes and moving toward the Middle Way. By concrete we mean that you or someone else could easily know when you've carried out an action step. They don't have to be grand in scope. It's even better when you keep the steps small. For example, in Debra's plan, she did not say she wanted to be more loving with Quinton, which is vague. She specified that she would hug him daily and kiss him good night. Those are good steps because they are both small and you would definitely know when they are carried out. We want you to develop your own action steps—plans that make sense for your particular situation. To give you some ideas, we have listed a few typical action items for finding the Middle Way of Parenting.

ACTION STEPS: THE ROAD TOWARD THE MIDDLE WAY

Schema	Example of Actions to Challenge Your Schema
Anxious-Attachment might cause you to: • Be overly involved in your kids' lives. • Not focus enough on your own life.	• Find an activity your children can enjoy by themselves or with other kids. Drop them off and have some alone time. • Develop an interest separate from your kids. • Make sure you have close, adult friends.
Avoidant-Attachment might cause you to: • Not feel close to your kids. • Ignore your kids' accomplishments.	• Hug your kids everyday. • Make a point of discovering what your kids do well and tell them.

Blameworthy might cause you to: • Feel like a terrible parent. • Feel it's your fault when your kids mess up.	• Remind yourself, you are doing the best you know how and you are taking steps in the right direction by reading this book. • Write down the Recipe for Child Development in chapter four to remind yourself that kids do what they do for many reasons, not just your parenting.
Blameless might cause you to: • Deny it when you make a mistake. • Blame others for your kids problems.	• When someone criticizes you, try to listen carefully. There may be some truth to it. • When your children have problems, look closely to see where the responsibility lies. Listen to what your kids' teachers and others have to say about the problems.
Naive might cause you to: • Give your kids too much freedom. • Not check up on your kids enough.	• Ask other parents, teachers, school counselors, or clergy for advice on what's reasonable for kids to do at different ages. • Know what your kid is up to. Meet your children's friends.
Distrust might cause you to: • Be overprotective of your kids. • Think the worst of everyone.	• Check with other parents to see what they allow their kids to do. Look at the evidence to see if they seem reasonable. If it seems reasonable, loosen up your restrictions. • Don't make instant judgments about your kids' friends. Again, check the evidence.

Other-Centered might cause you to: • Spoil your kids with material goods. • Do your kids' work for them.	• Pull back on what you give them. Buy presents only on special occasions and don't exceed a reasonable budget. • Make sure your kids have chores to do and that they carry them out. Don't rescue them.
Self-Centered might cause you to: • Resent your children for the time they take up. • Not provide your kids with the help they need.	• Find an activity you can enjoy with your kids. • Help your kids when they really seem stuck, but don't over do it either.
Perfectionistic might cause you to: • Criticize your kids too much. • Have overly high standards for your kids.	• Stop and think before you say anything critical to your children. Make sure it's important and necessary. • Praise your child about one thing every day. • Make sure your standards are set at an appropriate level for each child. Get information from your child's teachers if you're not sure.
Unambitious might cause you to: • Praise your kids for sloppy work. • Expect too little out of your kids.	• Make sure you only praise solid effort. • Know what your child is capable of and expect it. You can ask your child's teachers to find out.

No Play might cause you to: • Rarely have fun with your kids. • Devalue any activity other than productive work.	• Force yourself to go to movies or some other entertainment with your kids. Don't expect to enjoy it at first. • Allow your kids to have fun in the house even if they make noise or a mess.
All Play might cause you to: • Be your child's best friend. • Try and make everything fun.	• Remember, parents need to be leaders. Sometimes, to do that, you can't be a best friend. • Have regular chores for your kids; they will learn responsibility.
Excessive-Control might cause you to: • Discipline excessively. • Not allow your children to make their own decisions.	• Leave your kids' rooms alone unless they're doing something dangerous. • Deliver your discipline and consequences as emotionally neutral as possible. • Allow your kids to make some poor decisions when you know the consequence will only be modest. You want them to learn from their mistakes.
No Control might cause you to: • Let your children's behavior get out of hand. • Let your kids win battles over rules.	• Decide on a few important household rules and be firm and consistent. • Once you have made those rules, make yourself not back down. Remember, you're the parent and you set the rules.

We'd like to make two points about the action steps we listed above. First, you might have noticed that some of our steps broke our own rule about specificity. We made a few of them general so that you could use the idea and refine it to fit for you and your children. For example, allowing your kids to make some poor decisions is a little general. For your child, that might translate into not completing a science project ahead of time and suffering the consequence of a poor grade, or staying up all night to finish it. For some other parent, it may mean not reminding a child to put clothes in the hamper to be washed and suffering the consequence of wearing dirty clothes to school.

Many of the problematic parenting schemas can cause similar parenting problems and behaviors. For example, parents with *Distrust* or *Excessive-Control* or *Anxious-Attachment* could all end up overly restricting their kids, but for different reasons. You have to figure out what your schemas cause you to do. Therefore, you might choose an action step listed under one schema but apply it to a different schema. Thus, an *Other-Centered* parent might choose the action step we listed for *Anxious-Attachment* (i.e., "Develop an interest separate from your kids"). Again, these are merely ideas and possibilities. You have to decide what fits your schema and situation best.

SOCCER (Scoring Goals for the Middle Way)

Jennifer is obviously agitated and anxious. Pam sees the tension in her face. She barely gets a chance to greet her before Jennifer starts venting.

"Pam, I don't know what I'm going to do. Ever since last week, I've become increasingly ticked off at Jerod. I can barely walk into the house without blowing my top. It's been three weeks since he's been to school. He's made no attempt to get a job. I've tried to tell him he can't just hang around the house. But what do you do when a kid is six feet tall and over two hundred pounds? He ignores me. I can't imagine what consequence to give him. What am I going to do, ground him?"

"You're right, Jennifer, this is going to call for a new game plan. Jerod is too old to send to his room. It's a good time for us to play soccer."

"What? Hello, Pam. This is not funny."

"I'm sorry. I didn't mean to sound flip. I'm actually talking about a game plan for solving tough problems. It goes by the acronym SOCCER. It's a step-by-step procedure for dissecting problematic situations and creating solutions. Let me tell you what each letter stands for and then we'll go through them."

"Okay. Should I take notes?"

"Good idea. First, 'S' stands for *situation,* in other words the problem. This step defines and lays out the problem. 'O' is for *options.* Here, you brainstorm every possible solution. It's important to consider everything, including outlandish ideas. 'C' stands for *consequences.* You look at the likely consequences for each solution. The next 'C' stands for *choosing.* You select which option makes the most sense after considering the likely consequences. 'E' represents your *emotional* plan. I really like this step. Most problem-solving experts fail to appreciate the critical role of emotions in tackling problems. The best laid plans can be sabotaged by one's emotions, so it's important to prepare a plan for dealing with emotions. The final step, 'R,' is *rehearsal.* Some people like to call it role-playing. We practice carrying out the game plan. It's like the soccer coach having a scrimmage before the real game."

"Sounds great. I need to figure out what to do. Life with Jerod is becoming unbearable."

"Let's start with 'S.' Describe the situation."

"Well, Jerod is doing nothing with his life. He's sponging off me. And he's driving me crazy. I don't dare have anyone over to the house. I'm even afraid to stay out late for fear that he'll burn the house down with his cigarettes."

"I hear you saying there are several aspects to the problem. The first piece is that Jerod is not going anywhere in life. The second is that he's using up your financial resources. And finally, he's draining your emotional resources. Does that capture it pretty well?"

"Very well."

"All right. Now let's consider the 'O'—options. What are all the possible things you could do with this situation?"

"Well, I could tell him to get a job. But I've already done that."

"But that is one option. Let's consider the consequences— the first 'C'—of each option next. For now, we'll jot that one down. What other options are there?"

"I guess I could do what I'm doing now. I could pay his way and hope someday he'll change."

"Good. Are there any other possibilities?"

"I can't imagine doing it, but I could always kick him out of the house, never give him another dime, never speak to him again, and forget I even have a son. I almost did that before and in some ways I blame his current state on what I did."

"Yes. But, that remains an option. Can you also imagine an option that's a little less severe? Would it be possible to ask him to leave the house, but with some support. You could give him enough money for his first month's rent, invite him over for dinner once a week, and even pay for vocational training if he wanted it at some point. We could call it the Middle Way option. How does that sound to you?"

"It doesn't sound very middle to me—it still sounds too severe. But you said we should write down all the options. It's one of them, I guess. I doubt if it would work."

"That's all right. Can you think of any other options?"

"I could try to convince him to go back to school. Or I could let him stay at the house, but give him no money for anything at all. I would just feed him and provide a roof over his head. Those are the only options I can think of."

"Let me show you what we have so far. And we can add the consequences as we go. Then we'll choose the best one."

Situation

Jerod is going nowhere. He is draining me financially and emotionally. I can't even have a personal life.

Options	Most Likely Consequences
Tell him to get a job.	I already did this. Most likely he won't do it. He'll get mad at me and stay the same.
Status quo. Continue to give him money when he asks for it. Hope and pray he'll change.	He'll change when the earth stops spinning. I'll be angry and resentful. I don't think I could stand it.
Kick him out with no support. Forget he's my kid.	I can't do this. It would break my heart. I couldn't live with myself.
Ask him to leave, but offer him emotional support and transitional financial support.	He might ruin his life. Or he just might get his act together. I'd feel less guilty, but it would be very hard to do.

Options	Most Likely Consequences
Provide only food and shelter.	I would still have to put up with him invading my space. It wouldn't be good for him or me. He would still get the message that he doesn't have to work for a living. He might even steal from me. He's done it before.
Convince him to go back to school.	I've already tried this about a dozen times. He tells me to stay out of his business. There's no way he's going to listen to me.

"Pam, none of these options look very appealing to me. I don't think I can choose any of them."

"I'm afraid that's not possible, Jennifer. But we're at the second 'C'—choosing. You're choosing option two, the status quo, by trying to make no choice."

"And the status quo, I admit, is totally unacceptable."

"In that case, are there any other options that look intolerable?"

"I think providing him only food and shelter would be asking for major trouble. I really wouldn't put it past him to start stealing again. And I don't think he'd be motivated to do anything differently. I can also rule out options one and six because I've already tried them. They didn't work and there's no reason to think they will now."

"Well, Jennifer, where does that leave us?"

"I can barely stand to say this. But it looks like option four is the only one that has a chance of doing any good for Jerod and saving my own sanity. But how will I know he's going to be okay?"

Pam looks sympathetically at Jennifer, "I wish I could tell you he's going to be okay, but there are no guarantees, Jennifer. I know this is a terribly hard choice. But, as you said, it's the only one that *might* do him some good. And you need to have your own life. You're not abandoning Jerod this way. He's eighteen years old and you're still offering to be there for him. The choice is his."

"Okay, I know you're right. I just don't know how I can deal with it."

"That's why we have 'E,' the emotional plan. You know what to do in your head. Now we have to prepare you to handle your emotions. Without preparation, your emotions will sabotage the implementation of your plan. I want to offer you three tools for moderating emotions. The first is a breathing strategy which will help relax you. The second is learning to distract yourself from your emotions. And the last one is self-talk, a way to talk back to your emotions. Are you ready?"

"I'm willing to try."

"Now, Jennifer, I want you to close your eyes. Imagine your living room. It's smoky from Jerod's cigarettes. You turn off the television and tell Jerod you need to talk. What kinds of things do you think you'll feel when you ask Jerod to leave?"

"Panic. My heart's racing just thinking about it. I feel deep fear. I'm so sad."

"Keep your eyes closed. And stay in that scene. I want you to take a slow deep breath. Fill up the bottom part of your lungs first by pulling the air in with your diaphragm. When your lungs are full, hold the air for a few seconds. Then let it out slowly through your mouth, to a count of eight. You might find it useful to make a slight sound with the air to help slow it down as you exhale. I want you to do this three or four times."

Jennifer follows Pam's breathing instructions. Opening her eyes she remarks, "I'm surprised, but that does help a little."

"Good. This is a simple technique you can use any time you're feeling stressed. Practice it often and you'll get better at it. I've had clients who say a word or couple of words like tension out, let go, relax, or calm—as their breath turns from a breath in to a breath out. Now, I want to teach you distraction. Again, imagine yourself in the living room getting ready to talk to Jerod. Find an object just above his head you can focus your eyes on. It could be a spot on the wall, a lamp shade, or a picture. Stare at the spot and count backwards slowly from ten. You might think Jerod will wonder what you're doing. But, it's been my experience that most people don't notice what you're doing. They're usually preoccupied with their own thoughts. What spot in your living room did you choose?"

"Jerod's always on the couch. So I looked at the print above the couch. It's one of my favorite pictures. Distraction seemed to help a little, but not as much as the breathing."

"That's why we have several things to try. Now, let me tell you about self-talk. Have you ever seen one-year-olds learning about their surroundings? Infants depend on their parents to tell them what's right and what's wrong. Somewhere around the age of two, toddlers start to get it. And two-year-olds walk around saying, 'No. Don't touch," or some such thing in the voice of their parents. Later, they don't need to prompt themselves that way. The learning has internalized. That's sort of like self-talk. We come up with some useful things to say to yourself under duress. And we repeat them out loud a number of times. Later, you say them inside your head repeatedly. For example, you might say, 'This is the best option for Jerod. I'm not abandoning him.' Can you think of anything else to say?"

"I could say, 'I can do this. I must do this for everyone's good.'"

"Wonderful. You might want to spend some more time thinking about other useful things to say to yourself. Okay, let's review; we having a breathing technique, distraction, and self-talk to help you deal with your emotions. The last letter 'R' is for rehearsal. This is where we practice your plan."

"Is this like role-playing? I'm not very good at role-playing. They're always doing it at the staff meetings at work."

"It's more than role-playing. We're actually going to script the words you want to say to Jerod. Word for word. Doing this also helps control your emotions. So what exactly do you think you could say to Jerod?"

"I want to tell him I love him. And I want him to know that I want what's best for him. And that this is the hardest thing I've ever done. I'm going to say that he needs to find another place to live in the next three weeks. He's eighteen years old and it's time for him to grow up. I'll tell him I will help out with his first month's rent and deposit for a small apartment. He can come to dinner at my place once a week. And I'll lend an ear anytime he needs one. Later, if he decides to go back to school, I will help him with tuition and books. But he's on his own other than that."

"I've taken notes. Here's what you said. Now, let me be Jerod. And we'll practice."

"Okay. This feels strange, but I'll give it a shot. Jerod, I need to talk to you. First, I want you to know I love you. And I want what's best for you. This is the hardest thing I've ever done."

Pam interrupts, "Leave me alone, Mom. I'm watching a show."

Jennifer nods her head, realizing that's exactly what Jerod might say. She collects herself. "Now I might start my breathing. But, I'll continue. Jerod, you have to move out of the house. You are eighteen years old. It's time to grow up. I will give you money for your first month's rent and a deposit on a small apartment. You have three weeks to make arrangements and that's it. I would like to have you for dinner once a week here at the house. And I'm always here to talk to if you want. If you decide to go back to school, I'll help."

Pam, as Jerod, responds angrily, "How can you do this? I'm your only kid. You're selfish. You don't care about me."

"I love you more than anything, Jerod. This is the best thing for both of us. Nothing is going to change otherwise."

"I'm going to be homeless. I'll starve to death! How can you desert me like this?"

"Wow. That one's hard. Okay . . . Jerod, you are a bright young man. Other young men your age are able to find jobs. You can too if you want."

Pam, once again as Jerod, "I hate you. I never want to see you again!"

"I hope that's not true, Jerod. I'll always love you."

Pam, breaking out of her role, "I couldn't have said that better myself, Jennifer."

"Yeah, but I don't know if I'll be able to do it when Jerod is in front of me. I can see the value of practicing though."

"I know you feel that way. But I believe you can. It's a matter of memorizing and practice, practice, practice. Now, let's look at your entire SOCCER game plan. Take the plan and your notes. Practice on your own. Implement it if you're ready, but don't feel pressured to do so until you are."

JENNIFER'S SOCCER GAME PLAN	
Situation	Jerod doing nothing except draining his mother.
Options	Ask him to leave with temporary help.
Consequences	Jennifer can have her own life and Jerod has the best chance to turn his life around.
Choice	Jennifer will ask him to leave.
Emotional Plan	Breathing, distraction, and self-talk.
Rehearsal	Role-play, memorize script. Practice.

You can develop a SOCCER game plan for any problem you're experiencing with your child. This plan breaks down problems and their solutions into manageable steps. Watch out, though, your schemas might produce a lot of emotions urging you not to carry out your plan. But once you're convinced of the right choice, you can use your emotional plan and lots of rehearsal to prepare yourself. The SOCCER game plan can also be used to solve other life problems.

Jennifer left Pam's office, SOCCER plan in hand. She studied and rehearsed each component. Her anxiety increased her motivation and desire to get it over with. Her reluctance turned into resolve. She vowed to carry out her plan.

Friday after work, the living room is as she had imagined it in Pam's office. Dim light, stale smoke, television on a music video, Jerod lounging half-awake on the couch. Jennifer takes a few slow, deep breaths. Jerod doesn't notice her entry into the room. Bravely, she turns the television off and announces, "Jerod, we need to talk."

"Later, Mom. I'm watching TV."

"No, now. Jerod, first, I want to tell you how much I love you. And I want what's best for you."

"Time out, Mom. Please, no lectures. I've heard them all before. Enough already."

Undeterred by his remarks, Jennifer plunges on, "This is the hardest thing I've ever done. Jerod, you have to move out of the house. You're eighteen years old and it's time to grow up."

"What are you crazy, Mom? What am I supposed to do? I don't have a job. And I'm certainly not going to work at a fast-food restaurant."

"I will give you money for the first month's rent and a deposit on a small apartment. You have three weeks to . . ."

"Mom, stop. What are you saying? You can't throw me out on the street. I won't leave."

Jennifer focuses her eyes on the print above Jerod's head. She remembers looking at that same print for hours at a time while rocking Jerod as an infant. Sadly she continues, "Jerod, you have three weeks. You can stop by for dinner once a week. And I'm always here to talk to you if you want. If you decide to go back to school, I'll help."

"Mom? Mom, what are you saying? Mom, I love you."

"I love you, too, Jerod. That's why I'm doing this. You have three weeks. That's it."

Jerod's pleading, getting him nowhere, transforms into anger. "I'm sick of you, Mom. Enough. I'm not taking anymore of this shit! Fine. I'll leave. All you care about is yourself. I don't need you. I don't need your stupid dinners. I don't ever want to see you again."

"Jerod, I'm really doing this because I love you."

"That's bullshit, Mom. You don't love me." Tears stream from Jerod's eyes. "You couldn't do this if you loved me. And it won't be three weeks. Don't worry, I'm outa here tonight."

"Jerod. Jerod. Please don't leave tonight," Jennifer pleads. "We can work on this. We can make plans. I can help you."

"I don't want your help. I don't want anything to do with you." Leaping from the couch, Jerod angrily flings an ashtray at the wall. The frame of Jennifer's favorite print shatters.

She can hear doors and drawers slamming upstairs among sobs. Jennifer chants to herself, "I'm doing the right thing for Jerod. This is the right thing to do. I'm doing the right thing for Jerod. There was no other option." Sitting in the dark surrounded by broken glass, she hears the outside door slam. Without another word, Jerod has gone.

Practice

Flash cards are a great way to start tackling your schemas and the problems they create. Four-by-six index cards make a convenient format for recording this information. Of course, any kind of paper will suffice. First, fill in the label of the schema and its definition according to the way it applies to you. Use your own words. They might be a little different than the precise definitions we've given you. For example, you might use the schema label, "No Control." Our definition of No Control is "I can't say no to my kid. When I do make rules, I have a very hard time enforcing them, especially when my kid gets upset." Your definition might be, "I say no to my kids all the time. But they don't listen. And I cave in when they get upset."

Next, fill in the sensations and feelings you get whenever your schema is active. Remember, these are not thoughts. A few examples of feelings include anxious, mad, sad, glad, upset, irritated, angry, embarrassed, guilty, ashamed, etc. Sensations are feelings in your body. These can include: queasiness, tension, muscle aches, nausea, tightness in your breathing or chest, shakiness, tingling, or even a vague feeling in your gut.

Under "beginnings," record a brief synopsis of an event in your childhood that probably contributed to the development of the schema. For example, you may recall your mother or father fighting frequently and loudly. That might have scared you and helped create an "Anxious-Attachment" schema.

Then, think about the events in your life that set off your schema. Put some of those after the heading "Current Triggers."

The Middle Way of Parenting represents the balance you're trying to find. You probably know in your heart how you'd like to parent. That is the Middle Way. Reasonable, moderate parenting, with love and affection, as well as discipline as needed. It meets your child's needs without neglecting your own. You find the Middle Way by asking yourself how you can soften your schema-driven parenting without going to the opposite extreme. For example, if you have the No Play schema and work almost all of the time, the Middle Way would involve learning to plan times for fun, without abandoning your work ethic.

Action steps were covered comprehensively earlier in this chapter. You may wish to review that section for ideas.

Finally, try not to forget that everyone slips and slides on the path to change. We all have our ups and downs, much like the stock market. And like the stock market, change usually goes up over a long enough period of time. So be prepared to forgive yourself when you fall into the traps laid by your schemas.

SCHEMA FLASH CARD	
Schema Definition:	The Middle Way:
	Action Steps:
Feelings and Sensations:	1.
	2.
Beginnings:	3.
	4.
Current Triggers:	Self-forgiveness:

For times when schemas block your ability to find the Middle Way of Parenting, you might try SOCCER. Start SOCCER by describing the situation as clearly and concretely as you can. Then list all your options. Brainstorm. Ask friends for ideas. Even if the options sound ludicrous, write them down. Be creative. Take your time.

As you look at each option, consider the most likely consequence for each. Obviously, no one has a crystal ball. You can't *know* what's going to happen. But, with some thought, you can determine what consequence is most likely to occur if you follow through on any given option. So write that consequence down in the column provided.

SITUATION:	
Options	**Most Likely Consequence**
1.	
2.	
3.	
4.	
5.	

Now comes the hard part. Make a choice. Don't forget, if you make no selection, you've made a choice. The status quo. Thus, doing nothing should appear under options along with its most likely consequence. It *is* a choice.

The last two steps follow. First, make an emotional plan. Pam gave Jennifer a number of possibilities. You might try slow, deep breathing; distraction; or simple self-talk such as saying "I can do this" over and over in your head. Then, rehearse your option.

Imagine carrying it out and what you want to say and/or do. Try to think of as many possible reactions and outcomes as you can so you'll be prepared for them. Rehearse in front of a mirror or with a friend or therapist. You might even want to write out some of what you want to say like Jennifer did. Finally, you can summarize your entire SOCCER game plan on the following form:

Your SOCCER Game Plan	
Situation	
Options	
Consequences	

Choice	
Emotional Plan	
Rehearsal	

Chapter 8

TURNING THE CORNER

Improving Behavior in Yourself and Your Child

Active Listening

Kenneth settles comfortably on the couch in Dr. Brian Douglas' office. Previously, he'd always chosen the most uncomfortable, straight-backed chair in the office. His new selection does not go unnoticed by Dr. Douglas. Even Kenneth's posture appears more relaxed than in previous sessions.

Dr. Douglas offers, "Kenneth, would you like some coffee or tea?"

"As a matter of fact, Brian, coffee sounds good. With cream if you have it."

Kenneth's use of Dr. Douglas' first name provides evidence he's becoming more trusting and engaged in the process of therapy. "Sure. I'll be right back with it. While I'm gone, you can think about whether arguing the case has been helpful to you and if there's anything else on your agenda today."

Returning with the coffee, Dr. Douglas positions himself in the rocking chair opposite Kenneth. "So, how's it been going?"

"Overall, it's going pretty well." Stirring his coffee, Kenneth pauses. "I'm not sure how to put this. I've been searching for the right words. Really, things at home are quite a bit better. I've made progress in combating my schemas. I haven't been nearly as harsh or controlling. I've given the kids some space. I try to be less critical and usually I pull it off. And I can see that the kids are happier. At the same time, I feel sort of out of it. I don't know. It's really hard for me to describe. When I watch Nick and Lindsey with Sally, they seem so open and spontaneous. But they don't talk to me like they do to her. Am I making any sense at all?"

"Very much so. It's almost like you had a part in this family like a role in a play. Your role in the family was to serve as the judge and the enforcer. You critiqued everything and everyone. You set all the limits. Now, what is your role? What has it become?"

"Right." Kenneth leans forward, putting his chin in his hand. "That's it. I don't have a part anymore."

"How does that make you feel, Kenneth?"

"I'm sad. It aches. I feel lonely. I feel alone. I don't know if I've ever felt quite this way before. It's almost like I've lost my family. But it makes sense, what you said. I lost my part in the play. I don't know how to act."

"You said you never quite felt that way before, but does it remind you of any feelings in the past? Was there another time when you felt distanced from family?"

"You don't miss a thing, do you, Brian? You're right. I didn't feel connected to my family growing up. I was an outsider there too. What do I do now?"

"I think there are several things we can do. But first, before we start, I want you to realize you're not to blame for not knowing how to make better connections. You had no role models as a child. And as a parent, you were preoccupied with protecting and directing; you had no time to develop close relations."

"I get it. My Distrust and Excessive-Control schemas were so powerful they consumed my attention. They left no room for more meaningful connections with my family. As we've said before, my schemas get in my way, don't they?"

"Right. And now that you're chipping away at them, we need to replace your modus operandi with something else. A new skill. It's called active listening. It's really quite easy to learn. The hard part is using it."

"Like everything else so far." Kenneth smiles.

"True. Now let me describe active listening. It consists of four parts: validating, inquiring about feelings, probing, and last but not least, paraphrasing."

"Is paraphrasing where you repeat everything everyone says? I've done that at a communication workshop for attorneys."

"So, Kenneth, you're asking me if paraphrasing involves repeating back everything everyone says? And you're also saying you've done that at a workshop?"

Kenneth laughs. "And, Dr. Douglas, I am also saying that if you keep on doing that, I may have to find another therapist."

"I guess you like that technique as much as I do." Dr. Douglas laughs. "You can see exactly why people rarely continue to use this way of talking. It sounds artificial and it can get pretty damn annoying. The way I like to use it is a little different. You don't repeat back the entire message. At least not very often. With active listening, you find a part of what the other person has said and repeat it back in your own words for clarification. I usually use paraphrasing and validating together. By validate, I mean you find some piece of the person's statement to agree with or acknowledge. Let's try it out. I want to use a situation that might make you a little upset. One that would be hard to listen to. How about you be Lindsey and tell me why you want to go to an all-night dance?"

"Dream on, Lindsey. That's what I would say."

"I know, Kenneth. But I want to demonstrate active listening. You be Lindsey and I'm you using active listening for clarification or validation."

"Okay. So, I say, 'Dad, everyone in the universe—the whole universe—is going to this dance. Every other parent in the universe is letting their kid go. I want to go.'"

Dr. Douglas, pretending to be Kenneth, says, 'I realize you want to go, Lindsey. And it sounds like a lot of your friends are going. Is that right?' Now, do you see what reply does? It validated Lindsey's desire and showed understanding."

"Right, except, it doesn't get the job done. I still wouldn't let her go. I mean, I've loosened up a lot, but all-night dances are a bad idea. Aren't you just postponing the inevitable clash?"

"With active listening, it might not be a clash. If it is, it probably won't go down as badly. And what kind of response would you get from Lindsey with those questions?"

"She'd say, 'Yes, all my friends are going. That's why I have to go, and if I don't go, I'll never get invited to other parties.'"

"Right. And now I want to tell you about another part of active listening: inquiring about feelings. I would say to Lindsey, 'You sound worried about what your friends will think. Is that right?' Asking about feelings can change the tone of the discussion. It opens the way to sharing. You might be able to tell her how you feel as well."

Kenneth agrees, "I might be able to tell Lindsey how scared I would be if she stayed out all night. Maybe the two of us could work out a compromise."

"Precisely. Let's practice another one. I'll be Lindsey this time. How about if I say, 'Dad? I'm sixteen years old now and all my friends are driving. It's no fair that I can't drive, too.'"

"Okay. Lindsey, are you feeling frustrated about not being able to drive?"

"Good. You inquired about the feeling behind what I said. Now, I'll reply. 'Yes, I am Dad. I want to drive like my friends. You're always too protective.'"

Kenneth searches for words, "Lindsey, you want to drive and think I'm too strict?"

Dr. Douglas thinks for a moment. "Do you see how this technique would encourage Lindsey to speak? And how it can make her feel safer?"

"That's really what I want now. I want my kids to feel like they can talk to me."

"That's what we're working on. Now, let me add the strategy of probing. This is not cross-examination time. You especially have to be careful not to set up your kids to be criticized. This is not court. Can you think of some questions you might ask Lindsey to explore this issue further?"

"Well, I might ask her if she knows of any driving schools. And if she would be willing to call a few for details."

"You're probing and showing flexibility at the same time, Kenneth. How about we start a new topic and try out both of these techniques? I really like to tell my clients to ask a minimum of two questions prior to changing the subject or adding their own thoughts. More is even better. Let's say Nick wants to talk about his soccer game. I'll be Nick, 'Dad, I think I'd like to quit soccer. It's not that much fun.'"

"So, soccer's lost its appeal for you, Nick?"

"Yeah, Dad. I don't like it anymore."

"What don't you like, Nick?"

"I'm not very good. And everyone's always yelling at me."

Kenneth, out of character, says, "Brian, this would be the time when I would start criticizing the coach. I guess that's not the thing to do, huh?"

"You got it. By criticizing the coach, you don't get to learn what's going on with Nick. What else could you ask?"

"Well, he said everyone's yelling at him. I could ask him who's doing the yelling."

Dr. Douglas takes a chance. "You are Dad. I feel embarrassed when you do that."

"I'm not sure I like this active listening. I may find out more than I want to. But maybe I need to."

"I think you do, Kenneth. Now, how could you reply to Nick's last statement?"

"I guess I could say, 'I'm sorry, Nick.'"

"That might be good to say at some point, but with active listening, I want you to probe further. Ask more questions."

"Okay. So, Nick, when I yell at you, you feel embarrassed. Does that make soccer less fun?"

"Great, Kenneth. I think you understand. Do you see how asking that question will get to the real reason why Nick wants to drop out of soccer? Most importantly, it will let him feel safe to tell you. And consider the consequence of active listening. Yes, you heard something you didn't want to hear, but what do you think it might do to your connection with Nick?"

"That's obvious, isn't it? By the way, do you think that's the way Nick is feeling about soccer?"

"Maybe you should ask him."

"All right, I will. I want to know."

"Let me give you this card, Kenneth. It summarizes the active listening techniques we just covered."

Active Listening		
Action	**Steps**	**Examples**
Validate	Find a piece of what was said and agree or show support for it. This is particularly useful when you feel attacked or criticized. Your first instinct might be to argue or counterattack, but validating can deescalate conflict.	1. Sometimes that's probably true . . . 2. I can see how you might look at it that way . . . 3. That must be really hard for you . . .

Repeat	Restate part of what the person has said in different words. It's important not to overdo this strategy. Reserve it for two occasions. First, when you're really unclear about what the person is trying to say. Second, when there is obvious tension or anger. It helps to slow down the pace of the conversation and calm emotional turmoil	1. Let me see if I get what you're saying, "(repeat)" 2. Are you saying, "(repeat)" 3. I hear you saying, "(repeat)"
Inquire about feeling	Ask how the person feels about the topic of conversation and the process of talking about it.	1. So, how do you feel about that? 2. Is this hard to talk about? 3. Are you feeling (frustrated or angry) about this? (Use the feeling word you feel is appropriate here). 4. Are you upset with me about this?
Probe	Asks questions to explore the topic further. Don't offer your own opinion, tell the person what to do, or change the subject until you have asked at least *two probing questions*.	1. Tell me more about this. 2. Explain what you mean. 3. What do you think led up to this? 4. What happened next? 5. Help me understand this.

Before we return to Kenneth, we do have one crucial qualification to make. Active listening is *not* the thing to do when kids act inappropriately. When kids whine, pout, tantrum, or raise their voices, it's time to set limits. At those times, it's quite all right to boldly declare, "Because I said so!" or to simply to enforce a time-out or administer some other consequence. You are the parent and must determine when they've crossed the line. It's always okay for kids to register a complaint, discuss an issue, or express their feelings. It's all a matter of style and tone. When they are being appropriate, listen. When not, set limits.

Reinforcement

"Okay, Kenneth, I know we're covering a lot of territory in one session, but you're a great student. And I think you can absorb another concept. This one's also pretty easy on the surface."

"Yeah, like all your stuff. Easy to learn, hard to do."

"If there's one thing psychologists have learned, it's that people will do more of almost anything if they get rewarded after they do it. The trick is learning what each person finds rewarding or reinforcing. Some people only need a smile or a pat on the back. Others need more specific praise or compliments. And others only respond well to what we call tangible rewards. For kids, it can be candy or something small. For you and I, it might be money or gifts. You can figure out what people find reinforcing by observing or by asking them. Do you have any ideas about what Lindsey and Nick find reinforcing?"

"Sure. I think they both like praise. That's always been hard for me to do though. And Nick loves getting a new book. Lindsey is a typical teenage girl—she loves clothes."

"So, that's excellent, you've already identified ways to reinforce your kids. Now, is there anything you would like them to be doing more of that we can use to experiment with this rewarding technique?"

"I don't know, they mostly do what I want."

"Kenneth, what were we discussing when you first arrived today?"

"That I was isolated and felt disconnected from my family. But how can we use reinforcement for that problem? I don't see it."

"Well, people usually feel disconnected when the people around them aren't talking to them. I suspect you'd like the kids to talk with you more. That's what active listening was about, but you can help it along by occasionally reinforcing your kids for talking to you."

"You mean I should start paying my kids to talk to me? I don't think so!"

"No, no, of course not. Just let them know you appreciate it when they open up a little more. Say something like, 'Lindsey, I really enjoyed talking with you,' or 'Nick, I really like it that you took a risk and told me how you really felt.'"

"So, you think I should tell my kids I like to talk with them and that in itself will be rewarding?"

"Yes, Kenneth, your kids love you, and they crave your approval. Simply telling them you enjoy their company and ideas will be rewarding to them. If you want someone to open up, let them know you appreciate it when they do. Actually, there's a lot more about reinforcement and we may go into that later. But, the core of this theory is that people respond to rewards by doing more of what they were doing."

"I'm looking forward to trying these things out. I realize I don't do much rewarding with my kids, my wife, or for that matter, people I work with. I've always assumed that people should do what they're supposed to. I think it will be interesting to see what happens now that I am more aware of how I can influence others in a positive way."

"You know, Kenneth, sometimes you astound me. You're making an extraordinary number of changes. If I'm not careful, I might be out of a job."

Active listening is crucial for forming good bonds with your kids. When you paraphrase or validate a piece of what your children tell you, you are letting them know you have heard and understood. Asking questions lets them know you are interested in what they have to say. When you try active listening at home, like all new techniques, it may feel awkward. That awkwardness will fade with practice. Try not to forget to ask at least two questions before changing the subject or inserting your points.

Reinforcement is also a fundamental part of parenting. It's important to catch kids being good. They need to know when they are doing the right thing. This does not mean you should give empty praise. Don't tell your kids they did a wonderful job when you know otherwise. But when they at least make steps in the right direction, you need to tell them.

Entire books have been devoted to explaining active listening and reinforcement. As we said in the beginning, the intention of this book is not to offer basic parenting principles. You may choose to read more on these subjects, though you will do quite well by merely remembering to listen to your children and reward them when they do well.

After SOCCER Is Over: Self-development

Jennifer arrives at work, red eyes swollen from crying much of the weekend. Makeup fails to mask the dark circles under her eyes. Avoiding eye contact with her co-workers, she makes her way to her desk. After not eating in two days, her stomach now complains. But she has no appetite. Turning on her computer, Jennifer realizes she can't possibly concentrate. Sighing, she punches in Pam's number on the phone. Almost relieved, she gets her voice mail. She didn't really want to talk to a person anyway. She leaves a message, voice breaking, "Pam, it's Jennifer. I know you probably don't have time today, but I really need to see you as soon as you can work me in. Could you call me back?"

Pam hears the despair in Jennifer's voice message and finds time to see her at the end of her day. Upon arrival, Jennifer's appearance confirms Pam's hunch that she was in bad shape. Pam begins, "Jennifer, what happened? You sounded pretty upset."

Whatever measure of self-control Jennifer had gathered broke down as words burst forth. "I—I did it, Pam. I kicked him out. And I don't know if I did the right thing," Jennifer sobs. "I feel horrible. It was just like we feared. Jerod blew up, and Pam, he just stormed out. He left and I don't know where he is. He's been gone for three days and he hasn't called. I'm worried sick. I can't eat or sleep. Everywhere I go, I think I see him. Once I even called out his name." Her voice drops lower. "Pam, it's never Jerod. I feel like I'm going crazy."

"Jennifer, you're not going crazy. I don't know that you have lost your son forever, but even thinking you might have is a horrible, devastating thing to go through. Your reaction is natural; you're grieving."

"I know, it's almost worse than if he'd died. It's the not knowing that's killing me."

"That's right. And it's going to take time to get through this. First, we need to face your doubts about what you did. If you look back at what led us up to this decision, do you really feel there were any better choices? Is it possible we failed to consider a better alternative?"

"No, no, I've gone over and over this so many times, I

know there was nothing else to do. But, Pam, this is so hard. I can't stand it. I feel so depressed. How can I find Jerod and get him back?"

"I know that's what you want to do, Jennifer. But do you really think that would be good for Jerod? What message would that give him?"

"I don't know what the message would be, but what if he's homeless or in danger or something?"

"So, you think Jerod can't take care of himself? Does he need his mom to bail him out?"

"No, that's not what I mean. I know he has some friends and he's too smart to end up without food and shelter. His dad might even help him, I suppose. I just miss him so much."

"So, Jennifer, this is really more about you than him."

"I guess it is. How can I live without my son? He's my life."

"That's the problem. Now we need to find your own life. You've gone too long focusing exclusively on Jerod and neglecting your own needs. Of course, Jerod is very important. And when he was unable to look out for himself, you were always there. But now he's eighteen and can take care of himself better than you think. I know you don't want to do this right now. But I believe if we make some plans for your self-development, it will also cheer you up a little."

"Just being able to talk to you has helped some. But what kind of plans do you mean? Right now, I can barely get to work. I don't know if I can afford to spend the energy on anything else."

"You can't afford not to. Doing new things is going to give you energy, believe it or not. So tell me about your dreams, your hopes, your aspirations. What would you do with your life if you had no other responsibilities?"

"I don't know. I can't think in those terms right now."

"Yes, you can. Push yourself, Jennifer."

"Okay. Okay. You're being pretty insistent, aren't you? Well, let's see. I've always wanted to join a hiking club. I really like the outdoors. And I don't have a lot of friends. I sort of thought a hiking club would be nicer than one of those single clubs. You know, I'm really not looking for a guy. I've been alone too many years. But I do miss having adult company."

"Is there a hiking club close by? Do you know when they meet?"

"Actually, I do. I read those newspaper announcements. The hiking club meets the second Saturday of every month at different locations. I guess I could give them a call. But I really don't feel like it."

"I know you don't. But would you agree to call them anyway? And try going on at least three hikes?"

"Sure. Why not? I don't have anything else to do?"

"That's true right now. But didn't you tell me you've always wanted to go back to school and get a master's degree in business administration?"

"Well, yes. But it's been so many years. I don't have the computer skills that current students do."

"So, Jennifer, how you might get those computer skills?"

"Well, I guess I could always take a class or two at the community college. They're cheap. And they have a lot of night and weekend classes. Once I finished those, I could probably get into an evening MBA program."

"Wonderful. What's the next step?"

"All right already, Pam. I'll get a catalogue and check it out. But I hope you know how hard this is to do."

"Yes, I do. And I think we should meet regularly for a little while to make sure your depression doesn't get the upper hand. So, tell me again, what are you going to do this coming week?"

"I'm going to call about the hiking club and get a catalogue from the community college."

Self-development should not wait until after the children leave home. Jennifer had always focused too much of her life on Jerod. It wasn't good for Jennifer, and it wasn't good for Jerod. Again, the answer lies in balance, the Middle Way. That balance is individual. Some parents work many hours and stay connected with their children. Others prefer to stay at home with the kids for a number of years. There is no right or wrong way to achieve your own Middle Way.

In every case, the needs of the child predominate in the early years. Infants totally depend on their caregivers for survival. They consume almost every waking moment. Adolescents don't. As children develop more independence, so should parents. Try not to neglect your own development. You need to have your own focus and purpose. Doing so provides your children with a healthy role model.

Of course, sometimes modeling healthy behavior is not enough. A more direct approach is needed. We have already given you a few strategies for improving your behavior. First, Kenneth learned active listening and reinforcement. Mostly, he was attempting to foster a better relationship with his kids. Then, Pam taught Jennifer the importance of self-development. She needed to learn how to have a fulfilling life separate from her child's. Both of these parents were changing their own behavior, for their own good and for the good of their children.

Sometimes, turning the corner in your parenting involves targeting specific child behaviors (i.e., temper tantrums in the grocery store or fighting with siblings). It still requires parents to change their own actions. However, the actions are aimed at getting a child to behave in a different way.

Shaping: Getting Kids to Do More of What You Want

For Dr. Chavez, the rewards of being a school psychologist are sometimes subtle, which is why he's delighted with the obvious progress both Quinton and Debra have shown. Everyone at school is noticing positive changes in Quinton's behavior. He now looks forward to his appointments with Debra.

"Dr. Chavez, I've really been working with my schema flash cards and agitators," Debra gushes rapidly. "Quinton thinks I'm nuts, but we don't fight as much. But I'm stuck on a couple of things. He's working a little more on his homework, but it takes so much effort on my part to get him to do it that I'm getting worn out. I've already passed fifth grade, and it feels like I'm going through it again. And he still leaves his things all over the living room. But I really want you to know I appreciate all the help. Things really are a lot better. I don't want you to think I'm complaining. Like I said before, we don't fight as much and . . ."

"Whoa. Slow down, Debra. I'm glad to hear things are going better. How about we take these problems one at a time? It's interesting that these problems represent two types of challenges parents face. The first is getting kids to do more of what you want. The second is getting kids to do less of what you don't want. So let's start with the homework problem. Tell me what's happening."

"Well, Doctor, it all starts out about four-thirty. You see, Quinton gets home from school about three-thirty and you know, he's worked hard all day so usually I let him have a snack and watch television. Then at four-thirty I tell him to turn off the TV and do his homework. His response is always 'I don't have any,' or 'I'll do it later.' Every day. The same thing. Then I tell him to go get his book bag, which he does. Then I look at his notebook, which lists his assignments. He almost always has something to do. So we start.

I tell him to do it 'now.' He says, 'No.' I am doing better,

Dr. Chavez. I turn the television off and make sure he gets started. But if I turn my back for a minute, either the TV is back on or he's playing a video game. So we start again. Sometimes the cycle continues way past dinner. Frankly, I'm exhausted."

"Okay. Debra, what would this scene look like if Quinton did everything the way you wanted?"

"Well, he'd come home, have a snack, maybe watch a little TV, and do his homework without me asking. Or nagging."

"Right. Unfortunately, his current performance falls way short of your expectations. Rarely do kids ever make huge leaps at one time. What we need to do is move him one step at a time from where he is now to where you want him to be. I'm going to introduce you to a technique that behavioral scientists call *shaping*. It's a way we can get Quinton to do more of what you want."

"Sounds great. How do I do it?"

"First we need to establish the plan for getting Quinton where we want him. For example, we could chop this into three steps. Each step builds on the one before it. Therefore, each segment must be mastered before going onto the next. First of all, no TV until homework is started. Step one could be that at three-thirty when you ask, Quinton tells you the truth about what homework he has and gets out his books for fifteen minutes. Step two could be that Quinton works for thirty minutes, without reminders or prompting. Finally, Quinton does his homework completely on his own. Before you begin this program, tell Quinton exactly what he is going to do and what you are going to do. We'll even write it down on a chart for him."

"Good theory, Doctor. Now tell me, how do we get this miracle to happen?"

"Now you're going to get my two minute lesson on reinforcement and shaping. Everyone likes to get paid for what they do. That's what reinforcement is. A payoff. A reward. It would be nice if Quinton wanted to do his homework because he loves to learn, but the reality for Quinton is that he finds homework boring. Quinton alleviates his boredom by getting you to pay a lot of attention to him. By paying a lot of attention to him, you are in fact rewarding his misbehavior."

"But wait, it's not like I praise him for stalling and avoiding his homework."

"I know, but Quinton finds attention from you, any kind of attention, rewarding. So all the fuss over him is his payoff. His reward. That's got to stop. From now on, I don't want you to beg him to do his homework."

"But he'll fail. Won't that take us back to square one?"

"I doubt it, but we can expect some backsliding for a while. Believe me, keeping the TV off will, in itself, make a major difference in his homework efforts. Both attention from you and TV are rewarding for Quinton. So the first week, after he tells you what his homework is and works for fifteen minutes, he can watch TV for thirty minutes. After the fifteen minutes is up, let him know how pleased you are."

"But his homework won't be done in fifteen minutes."

"That's right and you're not going to worry about that. If he chooses to do more later, that's great and you'll reward him for that. But we have to make steps small. That's the essence of shaping. First, you define where you want to go—set a clear goal. Then, you break the process of getting there into small steps. So, after one week, you will expect him to work for thirty minutes before turning on the television. Then, the next week, he'll have to do all of his homework before a little TV."

"That's great, but I'm still the enforcer. I want him to do his homework without my involvement."

"That is the preferred goal. But let's face it. With Quinton, we're starting from scratch. No, worse than scratch. He's developed antihomework habits. We need to slowly shape new habits. Eventually, we will fade out your involvement, but for now, he still needs help. Let me ask you this, is there anything else that Quinton particularly likes? Something special?"

"He loves video games. He's always wanting the latest."

"Those can be pretty expensive, can't they?"

"Yes, but he begs and I usually give in."

"Not anymore. What's happening when you give in?"

"I guess I'm reinforcing him for begging."

"Yes. But, we'll use his desire for video games to our advantage. You know us school people can't resist charts. Let's sketch one out to use for this homework shaping project."

QUINTON'S HOMEWORK HELPER								
Goals	**Successes**							
I will start my homework for fifteen minutes.								
I will do my homework for thirty minutes.								

I will finish my homework without a fuss.							

Rewards

Every day I meet my goal I can watch TV for thirty minutes.

I get a sticker on my chart every day I meet my goal.

When I get twenty-five stickers I get to pick out a video game.

"Dr. Chavez, does this really work? It seems so artificial. So . . . I don't know, contrived?"

"Surprisingly, it does work. Mind you, things may get worse at first. That often happens when you start a program like this. What is most important for you, Debra, is that you remain firm and emotionally neutral. What I mean by that is that you need to matter-of-factly tell Quinton what you expect without begging, pleading, or harassing. And don't get upset, yell, or punish him if he doesn't do it. Let the consequences slowly work their magic. Believe me, they will in time. He will eventually discover the only way to get what he wants is to do what you want."

"So, what do I do if he turns on the TV without permission?"

"Unplug it. Don't argue or fuss. Again, emotional neutrality is the key. That one may be difficult for you, Debra, you're an emotional person."

"I can do it. But what if he takes the plug and plugs it back in?"

"No problem. You unplug it again and send him to his room for the rest of the evening."

"I'm afraid he won't go."

"Debra, I hate to put it this way, but you're still bigger than Quinton. This is exactly why we have to take care of this problem now—not when Quinton is sixteen. I'm not suggesting you'll have to use physical coercion, but it's possible you will have to lead him to his room a few times. Frankly, your stone-faced conviction will likely convince him to go without a huge struggle. Hear me one more time, firmness with emotional neutrality is key."

"Okay, I'll do it. Now, what about the mess in the living room?"

Response Cost: Getting Kids to Do Less of What You Don't Want

"The mess in the living room is something you want him to do less of, right?"

"Yes. He's like a little tornado. He stirs everything up and leaves a disaster in his wake. It seems like the second he gets home he starts messing things up. What can I do? I've tried nagging him to death."

"And that hasn't worked, has it? I'm not surprised. Nagging rarely does. Remember, Quinton likes attention of any kind. I think we need to fight this battle with different weapons. Tell me what kinds of things Quinton leaves around."

"His stuff. Video games, CDs, baseball cards, glasses, dishes, clothes, just about everything."

"Wow. We might have to use two techniques, both called response cost. They're called response cost because they teach kids that undesired responses or behavior will start costing them something they value. The first response cost strategy is for the things he cares about—the video games, CDs, and such. The other strategy is for the stuff he doesn't value as much, like dishes and clothes. Let me start with the first technique; it's easy. I want you to get a large garbage bag. You know, one of those you use when you're cleaning out your garage. Huge. Then, tell Quinton one time, calmly, that whenever you see his stuff in the living room, it will go into the bag for a week. Then do it. Don't talk about it. No nagging. Just do it."

"You're kidding."

"I guarantee this. It works even with the most difficult kids. I want you to focus on the items destined for the garbage bag first. Do it for three or four weeks. Live with the rest of it for a while. Once that's taken care of, you can deal with the dishes and clothes. You can't use the same method on these items because Quinton wouldn't care as much. You'd end up with a garbage bag full of dirty dishes in no time. You told me that Quinton gets an allowance. Sit down and tell him he may no longer leave his clothes and dirty dishes around the house. You are going to fine him a nickel for each and every item he leaves out that hasn't already gone into the garbage bag."

"He'll lose his entire week's allowance in a single day."

"He might, the first week. And possibly the second. But kids hate losing their allowance. Quinton isn't stupid. If you hang in there tenaciously, he'll come around."

With shaping exercises, such as Quinton's homework helper, you employ what you already learned about reinforcement, but you break the goal down into small steps or chunks. You reinforce each successful step until your child has mastered it. Use shaping when the goal is complex or difficult. Teachers use shaping all the time. For example, when learning handwriting, at first, a child is rewarded for making circles and lines. Later, the markings must approximate letters. Eventually, only legible handwriting is rewarded. Reinforcement and shaping will get your child to do more of what you want.

Response cost accomplishes the opposite, getting your child to do less of what you don't want. The technique involves taking away something your child values. You may have already heard of or even used time-outs. It's simply another response cost strategy. With a time-out, you tell children to spend a short period of time (usually about a minute per year of age) in a room where there's nothing to do. In effect, you are removing all fun and reinforcers from your child when you do this. Response cost strategies have been found to work more effectively and with fewer negative side effects than punishments such as spanking or yelling. A key in making response cost work is to implement it calmly, without emotion. Admittedly, this is hard to do. But it's more effective. On the other hand, if your little boy is running toward the middle of the street, don't fine him a nickel. Yell. Shout. And grab him as quickly as you can. Or if your little girl is about to burn herself on the stove, don't tell her to take a time-out. Again, intervene immediately, as dramatically as necessary.

But drama is not necessary for 98 percent of day-to-day teaching and discipline. For most of your parenting, active listening, reinforcement, shaping, and response cost will accomplish what you want. They are simple, straightforward techniques. Volumes of parenting books explain these techniques in minute detail. But the essentials appear in this chapter. The trick of parenting isn't learning these easily understood techniques, it's getting yourself to do them. And it's parents' schemas that make that task difficult.

Making Progress on Self-development

Jennifer worked hard on reworking her parenting schemas. She was able to finally set limits with Jerod. She wondered if it was too late. It might have been. Now she's learning to develop her own life, also an essential task for parents.

Opening her daily planner, Pam sees Jennifer's name penciled in for nine o'clock. She'd canceled her last two appointments and Pam was worried. Jennifer was ambivalent at best with her decision to tell Jerod to leave. Perhaps her resolve had wavered and she'd asked him back. Pam hopes not, for both their sakes. Jennifer arrives for her appointment on time.

Pam smiles in greeting her, discerning an improved appearance. The circles under her eyes have faded enough so that carefully applied makeup camouflages her distress. "How are you? What's been happening? I've been concerned about you since you canceled your last couple of appointments."

"I'm sorry about those, Pam. I should have left a more complete message. I didn't mean to leave you hanging. I guess it didn't occur to me that you would be worried. That's nice."

"I was just concerned because last time you seemed pretty depressed. Are you feeling any better?"

"I am. I'm sort of surprised about it, but I feel better. Not great, but better. I took your advice and joined the hiking club. I went on my first hike two weeks ago. It was okay. People were friendly and you won't believe this, but this guy asked me out. Of course, I said no. But then I saw him again on the next hike and afterward we had coffee. He was divorced a couple of years ago, and he seems really nice. I don't feel ready for dating yet, but it was nice to have someone to talk to."

"That's wonderful. You really are taking good care of yourself. Take all the time you need on that dating thing. No need to rush. You'll know when you're ready."

"You're right, and you'll be pleased to hear what else I did for myself. I enrolled in a business computing class at the community college. It starts in three weeks."

"Fabulous. I like what I'm hearing, a lot. By the way . . . I hate to bring up a difficult subject, have you heard from Jerod?"

"No. But his father called me and said Jerod's okay. My ex wouldn't tell me anything else. Hardly surprising from him. And Jerod still hasn't called me. That really hurts. I miss him so much. I still think I see him everywhere. Sometimes, in the grocery store, I imagine the person in front of me in the checkout line is him. I stare at him until he turns his face. It's stupid, but I always feel let down when it's not Jerod."

"Have you had second thoughts about what you did?"

"Yes, second, third, and fourth. But it was a relief to hear from his dad that he was okay. I figure if Jerod wants to talk to me, he'll call me. He's probably still really angry with me. I just hope he gets over it eventually. I don't know if he ever will. He needs to learn what adult life is all about. But sending him out like that, I don't know. He has so much to learn and he could get in awful trouble. And yet, I guess I did the only thing I could."

"Jennifer, you've made such progress in only two months. I know how hard this has been. You are one strong woman."

"I don't feel very strong. I still cry all the time when I think about Jerod."

"I'm sure you do. But you've done some very courageous things."

"Pam, you know what the hardest thing is? I can't stop thinking about all of the plans his dad and I made when Jerod was little. We imagined a happy family with Jerod growing up and going to college. I remember thinking of how handsome he would be going to his senior prom. And now there's no happy family. No college. Not even a senior prom. All those dreams—shattered."

"Now, Jennifer, I know this is horrible. But let's not give up. What you've done has at least given Jerod a chance. It's up to him now. And what we need to concentrate on is keeping you going."

"Don't worry about me. I'll hang in there. But it's really hard. Did I tell you about the picture? You know, the one above the couch. You taught me to stare at it to distract myself when I told Jerod he had to leave."

"Right. I remember. You said it had always been your favorite picture."

"Pam, when he left, he shattered that picture. He shattered it."

Practice

This chapter has covered a variety of techniques for changing children's behavior, including reinforcement, shaping, and response cost. Occasionally reward your kids when they do what you like and make sure there's a consequence when they do something you don't like.

We also covered something that's a little more difficult to learn—active listening. In a moment, you'll get the chance to practice active listening. But first, we need to remind you when you should use active listening and when you shouldn't. Kids deserve and need active listening whenever they are behaving appropriately, without whining, and speaking in a reasonable tone of voice. That does not mean they deserve to get what they want. You can listen and set limits at the same time. For example, your child may complain about not getting another dog. You can listen and explore those feelings, yet not give in to the request. However, if your child begins to whine, get louder, or use abusive language, end the discussion.

Even if what your children have to say is something you don't like, you can listen. But (and it's an important "but") when children are obnoxious and inappropriate, don't listen. And, above all, don't argue. Either call an abrupt end to the discussion, ignore them, or enforce consequences.

For more practice with active listening, try the following exercise. First, we'll provide an example of a common statement or request. Then, try to come up with a response from each of the active listening techniques.

ACTIVE LISTENING EXERCISE	
Statement	Active Listening
"Mom, I don't want to take piano lessons anymore."	Validate: Repeat: Inquire about feeling: Probe:
"I never get to stay out late like the other kids. It's not fair."	Validate: Repeat: Inquire about feeling: Probe:

(Write down something your child might say here.)	Validate: Repeat: Inquire about feeling: Probe:
"You make me sick! Why can't I spend the night at Jason's?"	Validate: Repeat: Inquire about feeling: Probe:

Did you fall into our trap on the last example? Remember, active listening should *not* be used when a child speaks inappropriately. A better response here is to simply say, "Because I said so!" Nothing more is required. You are the parent.

Chapter 9

FINDING THE MIDDLE WAY OF PARENTING

The Parenting Puzzle Solved

People buy self-help books because something in their lives isn't working. Undoubtedly, you were hoping to improve your parenting. You recognized your parenting wasn't going the way you wanted. Perhaps you found yourself disciplining too much or too little. Or maybe you felt a lack of connection with your kids. Whatever the specific problems, you wanted things to be better.

To deal with these problems many parents purchase books giving detailed advice on how best to parent. All too often, the advice sounds wonderful. And parents agree with the ideas, yet don't follow through. Now, we hope you understand why: the Parenting Puzzle. It isn't because they don't want to. Schemas cloud their vision and get in the way. Only when you understand and shed problematic schemas will you be able to parent with emotional intelligence and find the Middle Way of Parenting. At that point, you probably won't need a whole lot of advice.

Even if you do need some advice, first you need to tackle your emotional stumbling blocks—your schemas. Few people even know they have schemas, yet we all do. When schemas become extreme, they sabotage your best intentions. They create extreme moods, disregard contradictory evidence, put stress on relationships, and hurt children. They seduce you into doing too much of what seems like a good thing for your children.

The process of dealing with those stumbling blocks begins with an honest self-appraisal. Once you have identified your problematic parenting schemas, change has already started. Beware of the temptation to flip to the opposite extreme when you start to discern the problems your schemas are creating. If you do that, you'll end up where you started. As we said before, extreme opposites are as much alike as different.

The next step in taking on your schemas involves learning self-acceptance and responsibility. The focus on self-acceptance may seem to be another puzzle. It may sound like the antithesis of change to accept where you're at. But if you persecute yourself with guilt and shame, you'll have little energy for making changes. Often, reviewing your own childhood through a Lifeline will help you understand, and therefore accept, where your issues originated. This review is not intended to give you the message that it's okay to parent any way you like because you had a bad childhood. That's why we've moved beyond acceptance to responsibility. Accept yourself with all your flaws and foibles, then take responsibility for doing something about them.

Next we provided you with two techniques that lay the foundation for attacking your schemas. A cost/benefit analysis helps you identify reasons to give up your old, distorted patterns of thinking. It motivates you for the task ahead. The Self-Surveillance strategy helps you see more clearly how, what, when, where, and why your schemas operate. Turning the lights on schemas allows you to bring in the exterminators.

We presented two strategies directly aimed at exterminating distorted thinking and schemas. First, we taught you how to argue the case. Here we used information from your Self-Surveillance strategy and gave you a list of suggestions for strengthening your arguments. Second, the split-chair technique pits your problematic schema against the reasonable side of you. And everyone has a more reasonable side if they look for it.

The route to the Middle Way of Parenting followed. We helped you recognize a type of language we call agitators and how they stir up your emotions. Learning to moderate your agitators is crucial for finding the Middle Way. Flash cards also help you stay focused on the Middle Way. They tie up most of the ideas you've learned into one convenient package. And they contain action steps for finding the Middle Way. Finally, we recommended you start playing SOCCER as an approach to solving big problems. It gives you a way of finding the optimal, middle-ground solution and prepares you for carrying it out.

We concluded with various strategies for changing behavior (both yours and your child's). Once you have discarded your extreme problematic schemas, you'll find yourself emotionally equipped for carrying out these new behaviors. Active listening improves communication between parents and their children. This technique is useful in other relationships as well. Like active listening, reinforcement can be used both with your kids and others. When you reward people for doing something, they are more likely to do that something in the future. If you develop a habit of rewarding others, they begin to see you as a rewarding person to be with. That's all that reinforcement is, giving out praise, tangible rewards, and pats on the back for a job well done. We talked about self-development to remind you of the need for balance. A total focus on your children is unhealthy. It hurts you and it hurts your kids.

Misbehavior also hurts you and your child. When your child misbehaves, household tension increases. Our final two techniques target specific problems children frequently exhibit. The first is shaping, which breaks down big tasks into small steps. Each step in the right direction gets reinforced. Think of it as sculpting. You begin with a lump of clay and gradually form it into a piece of art. It's used to develop positive behaviors, things you want your child to do more of. And positive behavior pushes out misbehavior. You can also decrease misbehavior directly through response cost. Response cost teaches children that misbehavior leads to negative consequences, a loss of something they value.

Changing yourself changes your kids. It isn't so easy to do, but using the skills you've learned in this book can help make the task manageable. However, reading this book may not be the end of your journey to the Middle Way of Parenting. You may need to work through what we've given you a number of times. You may wish to use the exercises again and again. It may be helpful to discuss your endeavors in a group of other interested parents. You can form your own self-directed group by talking to other parents. Your school counselor could be a useful resource and might even help you form such a group. And you may wish to seek professional help. Most professionals would be comfortable with facilitating your efforts to work through the ideas in this book.

And what has happened with our families? As we said in the beginning, these families illustrate the major points we wanted to teach. Stories and parables are a highly effective method of teaching. Our families' problems may be more or less severe than the one's you experience. But the struggle is universal. And many families we've worked with have had problems much more profound than the ones we described. Whatever your particular family is like, you can benefit from these stories. That's because the process of change is the same for all of us.

New Beginnings

Kenneth, Sally, Lindsey, and Nick

The last family session. Dr. Douglas looks over his notes and feels hopeful. He remembers the first session with Kenneth and his family. Lindsey's crisis, as painful as it was, induced the family to seek therapy. Reflecting back, Dr. Douglas realizes it was Kenneth who worked the hardest at change. Dr. Douglas rises from his chair and stretches, anticipating a good session. Looking out into the waiting room, he's surprised by what he sees. Anticipation and hope transform into uneasiness and a sense of déjà vu. He notices Kenneth buried in a *Wall Street Journal.* Similarly, a book obscures Nick's face. Lindsey stares straight ahead. He can only see Sally clearly and she appears unnerved. Something's up. Dr. Douglas breathes a heavy sigh, "Good afternoon. Why don't you all come in?"

Kenneth carefully folds his paper and turns to Sally. He reaches out his hand for hers. "Are you ready?"

Sally takes his hand and smiles affectionately. "Sure, honey. Come on, kids."

Now thoroughly confused, Dr. Douglas watches Lindsey and Nick who show no signs of tension or reluctance. The family settles into Dr. Douglas' inner office. "What's up? How's it going?"

"Great," Kenneth speaks. "Those last two things you taught me have been amazing. Active listening and reinforcement really work. I feel like part of this family again. I'm still struggling some, but I can't tell you how much things have changed."

Dr. Douglas turns to Sally. "Would you agree with Kenneth's assessment?"

"Agree? Are you kidding? It's like he's a different person and our marriage hasn't been this good in fifteen years. We're talking again."

Dr. Douglas grins. "You know, I have a confession to make. When I looked out at you all in the waiting room, I thought for a moment that we hadn't accomplished much. I saw Kenneth and Nick buried in their reading and I imagined distress on Sally's and Lindsey's faces. The scene resembled the first time I saw your family. I guess it triggered my own Perfectionist schema. If everything doesn't look idyllic, I sometimes assume the worst. That one still catches me every now and then. See how powerful those things can be?"

Kenneth nods and grins. "So, even the great Dr. Douglas gets snared by schemas? I kinda like hearing that, Brian. If someone who knows this stuff as well as you do can fall prey to schemas, I guess I don't have to feel so bad."

Sally adds, "Yes, Dr. Douglas, I wasn't upset at all. I was really just trying to remember what I needed to buy at the grocery store. It is comforting to know we're not the only ones who get tripped up by schemas."

"That's why I confessed," Dr. Douglas admits. "The main thing is, I'm glad the family seems to be doing better. And how about Lindsey and Nick? Do you two agree with your parents' evaluation?"

Lindsey, with less enthusiasm than her mother, replies, "Well, Dad's getting better. No doubt about it. But he's still too strict and he can't stop himself from yelling sometimes. Although I do think he tries not to."

Dr. Douglas looks to Nick who remains silent. "Nick? What's your take on things?"

"Sure, it's been a whole lot more peaceful around the house. Dad's not yelling at my soccer games. And Mom seems a lot happier. I just don't know how long this is going to last. I worry . . . I worry . . . I don't know. I just don't know if everything will hold together."

Sally leans toward Nick. "Oh sweetie, you don't need to worry. We're going to be fine."

Before Dr. Douglas gets a chance to comment, Kenneth looks at Nick. "Nick, apparently you feel things are better, but you're worried how long it will last. Tell me more about your concerns."

Dr. Douglas feels like a proud teacher watching his star pupil perform. Kenneth and Nick continue their dialogue as the rest of the family looks on.

Nick begins slowly, "I don't know, Dad. It's just that I was so scared when you and Mom were mad at each other. And it scared me too when Lindsey ran away. I felt all alone. I don't ever want it to be that bad again."

"Did you feel alone because there was no one to talk to?"

"Yeah, I couldn't talk to Mom. She was so sad, I didn't want to bother her with my troubles. And you would have thought I was a wimp. I could never talk to you."

"Is it getting any easier to talk to me now? If it's not, I want to know."

"Yeah. But it's hard to trust you. I think you might start your yelling again. Sometimes you still do."

"I know. And I'm sorry about that, Nick. I am really trying. I can't tell you how much it hurts me to think about all of the conversations I might have been able to have with you if I hadn't been so harsh." Kenneth turns to Sally and Lindsey. "And all the conversations I missed with you, Lindsey, and you, Sally." With tears in his eyes, Kenneth proceeds, "I want you all to know, and especially you, Nick, talking with you lately has brought me more joy and meaning than anything else in my life. I want us to be close and I know it will take time for you to trust that."

Quinton and Debra

On the night of Quinton's fifth-grade graduation, Debra checks her hair in the mirror one more time. Satisfied, she calls to Quinton, "Are you ready? We need to leave right now." No answer. "Quinton, let's go." Still not hearing a reply, Debra finds him in his room, engrossed in a video game. "Quinton, I told you a half an hour ago to be ready. Get your new jacket and tie on now."

"Just a minute, Mom. I'm almost at the next level."

Debra unplugs the game from the television. "This goes in the black bag for a week. Now, get ready."

"Mom. That's not fair. You didn't tell me I'd lose my video games."

"Life isn't fair, Quinton. Get ready now or lose something else," Debra calmly states as she walks out of his room. "I'll be in the car." Debra goes to the car to wait and reflects on how nice it's been not to have to do battle with Quinton very often anymore. And when conflict arises, it's short-lived.

Arriving at the elementary school, Debra parks the car. She sees all of the families piling out of their cars—moms, dads, children, grandmothers, grandfathers, and other relatives. She feels a pang of envy. So many school events she attends alone. Her husband is usually out of town or working late. Holding her head up, she and Quinton enter the school building and head for the auditorium. Quinton goes to sit with his class while Debra takes a seat by herself. The auditorium is noisy with people greeting each other. Debra feels uncomfortable, not just from the stuffiness of the room, but because she knows so few people. She's never been an active participant in school committees and rarely volunteered. She thinks to herself, "Maybe I didn't get involved because I was really embarrassed by Quinton's behavior. I was always blaming the school. I think that was a mistake. Maybe next year I'll help out a little more."

The auditorium quiets as Principal Pat Hansen begins to speak, "Welcome, students, parents, families, and friends . . ."

After forty-five minutes of speeches, Debra's attention drifts to thoughts about her life. She's approaching forty. On the one hand, she feels optimistic about Quinton. And she feels a new sense of competence and purpose as a mother. On the other hand, she feels isolated and unfulfilled. Her expensive dress, fancy car, and beautiful home no longer satisfy her. She yearns for meaning and intimacy. Something's got to change. Dr. Chavez suggested marital therapy a few weeks ago. And he said I should go with or without my husband. I think I will.

"Sandy Adams," the principal calls out. "Sandy has been awarded the master math award given to the student who scores the highest on our fifth-grade achievement test. I must say that I am especially pleased to have a young lady excel in mathematics. Sandy, congratulations." Applause ripples through the auditorium.

Debra's hands become clammy as she apprehensively anticipates the names of the sixty-five fifth-graders being called one at a time. It seems like every child is getting some sort of award. Honor roll, sports awards, student of the month or year, on and on. Each time a name is called, enthusiastic families and friends applaud. Debra dreads the calling of Quinton's name, knowing she is his only fan and that he won't get any recognition. For the first time, Debra realizes how hard it must be for Quinton. Before therapy, her only concern would have been her own embarrassment. Now she aches for her son. No wonder he was less than enthusiastic about getting ready on time.

"Martha Kaser," Pat Hansen calls. "Martha, I am pleased to present you with the sociability award given to the student voted as the friendliest of all the fifth grade." The audience cheers. "Geoffrey Kyle. Geoffrey has had a very successful year and receives one of our good attendance awards."

Scattered applause. Debra thinks, "Well, at least every student is not wildly popular." But anxiety still sits in her stomach. The names continue. Debra loses track of the proceedings. After an hour and a half, it's clear the audience is getting restless. Children are starting to talk and misbehave. Toddlers can be heard whining.

Pat Hansen asks for quiet. "Please, ladies and gentlemen. We are almost finished. I don't want you to miss this next student. First, I need to say that this student is very special to me. I have spent many hours with this child since first grade. Some positive, but frankly, many more not so positive. Rarely, in my twenty years as an educator, have I witnessed such a dramatic improvement in a student. In a unanimous vote, our faculty overwhelmingly agreed on the most improved student of the year. It is with great pleasure that I announce our winner, Quinton Valenski, most improved student of the year."

Startled, Debra gasps. Dr. Chavez, seated on stage, stands, leading the applause. Quinton's fifth-grade faculty also rise, followed by the entire auditorium. Quinton runs across the stage into the arms of Pat Hansen.

Jennifer and Jerod

Jennifer hates the time of year when darkness arrives by five o'clock. It makes her want to go home, curl up on the couch, watch TV, and go to bed early. As she drives into the community college parking lot a little late for her class, second thoughts materialize. She thinks, "Maybe I should never have signed up for this class. I don't feel like going. I'm so tired; besides, I'm late. Can I really make it through an entire semester of this? Well, I'll go to the first class and see. I can always drop it."

Overall, Jennifer knows she's doing better. She's been active in the hiking club and has made a few friends. For the most part, her depression has lifted. Walking briskly down the hall she hesitates in front of the rear door to the classroom. "Well, here goes. I got this far, I might as well go in. I'll sit in the back."

She finds a seat in the back row of the computer lab. Fortunately, the instructor doesn't seem to notice her late arrival. He continues his lecture, "As I said at the beginning, this is not a class for novice computer users wanting to learn word processing. I expect all students to be somewhat familiar with PCs and their operating system. We'll be working on advanced spread sheets and other business applications. Are there any questions?"

A young man in the second row raises his hand and asks a question Jennifer can't quite make out. Watching, she thinks, "My God, that's Jerod! It looks just like him. It even sounds like him. But it can't be him. I'm always doing this. I must be going crazy. And here I thought I was getting better. What's wrong with me?"

The instructor answers the young man's question about lab hours and reviews the course syllabus and objectives in detail. Unable to concentrate, Jennifer decides to leave at the end of class and drop the course. "I'm not ready yet," she thinks. "I need to give myself more time." Her thoughts turn to Jerod and the enduring grief that haunts her. She is surprised by the rapid passage of time, and startled when the other students collect their belongings in preparation to go home. Not wishing to be noticed, she quickly exits through the rear door. Head down, she darts along the hallway. "Oh, excuse me. I'm sorry," she exclaims as she collides into a student coming out of the other door.

"Mom? Mom? What are . . ."

"Jerod! It is you?"

"What do you mean? Of course, it's me."

"I—I was sitting in the back. I thought it was you, then I thought I was imagining things. How are you? Are you okay? What are you doing in this class? It's so good to see you. Where are you living? Are you okay?"

"Wait. Hold on, Mom. I'm okay. I'm doing fine. What are you doing in this class? Hey, Mom, how about I buy you a cup of coffee? You got time? We could go to the student union."

"Oh, Jerod, I have lots of time." Jennifer drops her books in eagerness to pull Jerod into her arms.

"Mom. Not here. Come on, let's go have some coffee."

Seated with steaming lattes on the table, Jennifer says, "Jerod, I didn't even know you liked coffee."

"There's a lot about me you don't know, Mom."

"It's good to see you, Jerod. I've missed you so much. Why haven't you called?"

"I couldn't. At first, I was mad. I wanted to punish you. Later, I felt ashamed. Mom, I wasn't a good son. I was lazy and I used you. I can see that now."

"Oh, Jerod. Don't talk like that. A lot of it was my fault. I know that now."

"Well, you did the right thing, Mom. I needed to learn a lesson. Kicking me out was the only way I could learn. I wanted to wait and call you when I had made something of myself. I dreamt about one day driving up to the house in my own car and taking you to a fancy restaurant. I guess I'm not quite there yet."

"You didn't have to wait, Jerod. And here you sit. You're going to school, and this coffee is better than any fancy restaurant. Tell me how you got here."

"It was pretty grim at first. I stayed with some friends for a few weeks. I got a job at a convenience store. I hated it. You wouldn't believe the sleazy characters who show up in those places. Late at night I went from being scared I'd be robbed to bored out of my mind. So, I started looking around and got a job as a salesperson at a computer store. The manager really liked me. And I got to be pretty good at the ins and outs of computers."

"Jerod, that's wonderful. Are you still working there?"

"Yeah, it doesn't pay a whole lot. But the manager, she's great about my hours. She let me arrange time to go to G.E.D. classes and, Mom, I passed it on my first try. It took me only four weeks to study for it."

"Wow. Well, we always knew you were smart. So, my son has finished high school. I'm proud of you, Jerod."

"That's only the beginning. The store pays for my college classes as long as I get B's. That's no problem. I've finished two courses with A's in both of them. I want to get a degree in computer science."

"I can't believe this is you talking, Jerod. I'm stunned. Where are you living?"

"That's the bad news. I've got a tiny studio around the corner. It's all I can afford. You wouldn't believe it, Mom. The refrigerator is about a hundred years old, only one burner works on the stove, and the place was filthy beyond belief when I moved in. I've cleaned it up, but there's still roaches. It's gross."

"Oh, Jerod. You can't live like that. I'll help you out. Let me give you a couple hundred dollars a month. Or better yet, come home."

"Mom, thanks. But, no way. I've got to do this myself. You showed me that. I feel better about myself than I ever have. And that's because you made me."

"Jerod, I am so proud of you. You are everything I'd dreamed. You are the son I've always wanted. If you won't take my help, will you at least have dinner with me after class next week?"

"Of course, sure, Mom, that would be great."

"Jerod, it's late. I hate to go. Thanks for the coffee. I'll see you in class."

"Mom . . . Mom, I love you."

RESOURCES

Adams, Christine, and Ernest Fruge. 1996. *Why Children Misbehave and What to Do about It*. Oakland, Calif: New Harbinger Publications. This book offers strategies for solving problems with tantrums, sassiness, aggression, and other common childhood problems.

Beck, Aaron T. 1976. *Cognitive Therapy and the Emotional Disorders*. New York: International Universities Press. Dr. Beck, the founder of cognitive therapy, presents the theoretical basis and philosophy of this approach as applied to a wide range of problem areas. Intended for professionals, Beck's book is considered a classic in the field. Our book on parenting expands upon, but is quite consistent with, the principles and philosophy of cognitive therapy.

Brazelton, T. Berry. 1994. *Touchpoints: Your Child's Emotional and Behavioral Development*. Reading, Mass.: Perseus Press. Dr. Brazelton is a well-known pediatrician whose writings on infancy and early childhood provide wonderful overviews of child development.

Clark, Lynn F. 1996. *SOS: Help for Parents*. Berkeley, Calif.: Parents Press. Dr. Clark uses behavior modification principles for teaching parents how to manage problematic child behavior. His book distills this information in an exceptionally easy to understand format.

Elliott, Charles H., and Maureen Kirby Lassen. 1998. *Why Can't I Get What I Want?: How to Stop Making the Same Old Mistakes and Start*

Living a Life You Can Love. Palo Alto, Calif.: Davies-Black.
This book is intended for readers interested in learning more about how schemas affect every part of their lives and what to do about it. Includes ideas from chaos theory and Zen, integrated with cognitive therapy.

Faber, Adele, and Elaine Mazlish. 1991. *How to Talk So Kids Will Listen and Listen So Kids Will Talk.* New York: Avon Books.
This classic book provides a step-by-step approach to improving communication between parents and children.

Lassen, Maureen Kirby. *Why Are We Still Fighting? How to End Your Schema Wars and Start Connecting with the People You Love.* Oakland, Calif.: New Harbinger Publications, in press.
The schema model applied to relationships and how to change destructive patterns.

McKay, Gary, and Don Dinkmeyer. *1997. The Parent's Handbook: Systematic Training for Effective Parenting.* New York: Random House.
The authors present parenting techniques based on a nationally successful parenting program.

McKay, Matthew, Kim Paleg, Patrick Fanning, and Dana Landis. 1996. *When Anger Hurts Your Kids.* Oakland, Calif.: New Harbinger Publications.
This book teaches parents to learn more about the beliefs behind their anger and find alternatives.

Rosemond, John. 1991. *Parent Power: A Common Sense Approach to Parenting in the '90s and Beyond.* Kansas City, Mo.: Andrews and McMeel.
The author has written extensively in the area of parenting. This book helps parents anticipate typical problems. We agree with his view that most parents already know what's best for their children.

Young, Jeffrey E., and Janet S. Klosko. 1993. *Reinventing Your Life: How to Break Free from Negative Life Patterns.* New York: Dutton.
Well-written, clear, and interesting. Largely focused on how schemas affect fairly severe, ingrained problems.

Laura L. Smith, Ph.D. has Masters degrees in both Special Education and clinical psychology. She obtained her Ph.D. in Clinical Psychology in 1997. She taught parenting and special education for ten years and is now a school psychologist with Albuquerque Public Schools. She also works privately as an educational consultant.

Charles H. Elliott, Ph.D. obtained his Ph.D. in Clinical Psychology in 1976. He has served on the faculties in the psychiatry department at the University of Oklahoma Health Sciences Center and at the University of New Mexico School of Medicine. In addition, he has written numerous articles and book chapters in the area of cognitive-behavior therapies and pediatric psychology. Currently, he has a private practice in clinical psychology and is a faculty member at the Fielding Institute. He is the co-author of one self-help book, *Why Can't I Get What I Want?* (Davies-Black, 1998; a Behavioral Science Book Club Selection).

More New Harbinger Titles
for Parents and Families

KID COOPERATION
How to Stop Yelling, Nagging, and Pleading and Get Kids to Cooperate

There really is a way to talk so that kids will listen and be reinforced to be helping, responsive members of the family. This is an empowering work, filled with practical skills.   *Item COOP $13.95*

UNDERSTANDING YOUR CHILD'S SEXUAL BEHAVIOR

Puts parents' minds at ease by describing common behaviors and contrasting those that are a normal part of exploration and play with those that may indicate a need for help.   *Item CSB $12.95*

CHILDREN CHANGED BY TRAUMA

The first book to show parents what they can do to help a child who has experienced a traumatic event deal with the experience.   *Item CCT $13.95*

WHY CHILDREN MISBEHAVE
And What to Do About It

This text offers practical strategies for dealing with common behavior problems in a concise, easy-to-use format. Beautifully illustrated by over 100 photographs.   *Item BEHV $14.95*

WHEN ANGER HURTS YOUR KIDS
A Parent's Guide

Learn how to combat the mistaken beliefs that fuel anger and how to practice the art of problem-solving communication—skills that will let you feel more effective as a parent and let your kids grow up free of anger's damaging effects.   *Item KNOW $12.95*

Call **toll-free 1-800-748-6273** to order. Have your Visa or Mastercard number ready. Or send a check for the titles you want to New Harbinger Publications, 5674 Shattuck Avenue, Oakland, CA 94609. Include $3.80 for the first book and 75¢ for each additional book to cover shipping and handling. (California residents please include appropriate sales tax.) Allow four to six weeks for delivery.

Prices subject to change without notice.

Some Other New Harbinger Self-Help Titles

The Self-Esteem Companion, $10.95
The Gay and Lesbian Self-Esteem Book, $13.95
Making the Big Move, $13.95
How to Survive and Thrive in an Empty Nest, $13.95
Living Well with a Hidden Disability, $15.95
Overcoming Repetitive Motion Injuries the Rossiter Way, $15.95
What to Tell the Kids About Your Divorce, $13.95
The Divorce Book, Second Edition, $15.95
Claiming Your Creative Self: True Stories from the Everyday Lives of Women, $15.95
Six Keys to Creating the Life You Desire, $19.95
Taking Control of TMJ, $13.95
What You Need to Know About Alzheimer's, $15.95
Winning Against Relapse: A Workbook of Action Plans for Recurring Health and Emotional Problems, $14.95
Facing 30: Women Talk About Constructing a Real Life and Other Scary Rites of Passage, $12.95
The Worry Control Workbook, $15.95
Wanting What You Have: A Self-Discovery Workbook, $18.95
When Perfect Isn't Good Enough: Strategies for Coping with Perfectionism, $13.95
Earning Your Own Respect: A Handbook of Personal Responsibility, $12.95
High on Stress: A Woman's Guide to Optimizing the Stress in Her Life, $13.95
Infidelity: A Survival Guide, $13.95
Stop Walking on Eggshells, $14.95
Consumer's Guide to Psychiatric Drugs, $16.95
The Fibromyalgia Advocate: Getting the Support You Need to Cope with Fibromyalgia and Myofascial Pain, $18.95
Healing Fear: New Approaches to Overcoming Anxiety, $16.95
Working Anger: Preventing and Resolving Conflict on the Job, $12.95
Sex Smart: How Your Childhood Shaped Your Sexual Life and What to Do About It, $14.95
You Can Free Yourself From Alcohol & Drugs, $13.95
Amongst Ourselves: A Self-Help Guide to Living with Dissociative Identity Disorder, $14.95
Healthy Living with Diabetes, $13.95
Dr. Carl Robinson's Basic Baby Care, $10.95
Better Boundries: Owning and Treasuring Your Life, $13.95
Goodbye Good Girl, $12.95
Fibromyalgia & Chronic Myofascial Pain Syndrome, $19.95
The Depression Workbook: Living With Depression and Manic Depression, $17.95
Self-Esteem, Second Edition, $13.95
Angry All the Time: An Emergency Guide to Anger Control, $12.95
When Anger Hurts, $13.95
Perimenopause, $16.95
The Relaxation & Stress Reduction Workbook, Fourth Edition, $17.95
The Anxiety & Phobia Workbook, Second Edition, $18.95
I Can't Get Over It, A Handbook for Trauma Survivors, Second Edition, $16.95
Messages: The Communication Skills Workbook, Second Edition, $15.95
Thoughts & Feelings, Second Edition, $18.95
Depression: How It Happens, How It's Healed, $14.95
The Deadly Diet, Second Edition, $14.95
The Power of Two, $15.95
Living Without Depression & Manic Depression: A Workbook for Maintaining Mood Stability, $18.95
Couple Skills: Making Your Relationship Work, $14.95
Hypnosis for Change: A Manual of Proven Techniques, Third Edition, $15.95
Letting Go of Anger: The 10 Most Common Anger Styles and What to Do About Them, $12.95
Infidelity: A Survival Guide, $13.95
When Anger Hurts Your Kids, $12.95
Don't Take It Personally, $12.95
The Addiction Workbook, $17.95
It's Not OK Anymore, $13.95
Beyond Grief: A Guide for Recovering from the Death of a Loved One, $14.95
The Chemotherapy & Radiation Survival Guide, Second Edition, $14.95
An End to Panic: Breakthrough Techniques for Overcoming Panic Disorder, Second Edition, $18.95
Dying of Embarrassment: Help for Social Anxiety and Social Phobia, $13.95
The Endometriosis Survival Guide, $13.95
Grief's Courageous Journey, $12.95
Flying Without Fear, $13.95
Stepfamily Realities, $14.95
Coping With Schizophrenia: A Guide For Families, $15.95
Conquering Carpal Tunnel Syndrome and Other Repetitive Strain Injuries, $17.95
The Three Minute Meditator, Third Edition, $13.95
The Chronic Pain Control Workbook, Second Edition, $17.95
The Power of Focusing, $12.95
Living Without Procrastination, $12.95
Kid Cooperation: How to Stop Yelling, Nagging & Pleading and Get Kids to Cooperate, $13.95